# EFFECTIVE COUNSELING

**Psychology for Church Leaders Series**

# EFFECTIVE COUNSELING

### Gary R. Collins

*CREATION HOUSE*
**CAROL STREAM, ILLINOIS**

Other books in the
Psychology for Church Leaders Series

*Man in Transition*
*Fractured Personalities*
*Man in Motion*

Published by Creation House,
499 Gundersen Drive, Carol Stream, Illinois 60187.
In Canada: Beacon Distributing Ltd.,
104 Consumers Drive, Whitby, Ontario L1N 5T3.

First Printing—May, 1972
Second Printing—November, 1973
Third Printing—August, 1974
Fourth Printing—March, 1976

International Standard Book Number 0-88419-022-6
Library of Congress Catalog Card Number 79-189628

# ACKNOWLEDGMENTS

The author gratefully acknowledges the cooperation of the following publishers who have given written permission to quote from the sources listed below:

Abingdon Press—For excerpts from Rollo May, *The Art of Counseling,* Copyright 1939; S. Hiltner, *Pastoral Counseling,* Copyright 1949; and Howard J. Clinebell, Jr., *Basic Types of Pastoral Counseling,* Copyright 1966.

Allyn and Bacon, Inc.—For excerpts from J. F. Adams, ed., *Understanding Adolescence:Current Developments in Adolescent Psychology.* Copyright 1968.

Basic Books, Inc.—For excerpts from M. Jahoda, *Current Concepts of Positive Mental Health,* Copyright 1958.

Broadman Press—For excerpts from Wayne Oates, *An Introduction to Pastoral Counseling,* Copyright 1959.

*Christianity Today*—For excerpts from R. J. Hastings, "Are Funerals Dying Out?" Nov. 22, 1968.

Doubleday & Co., Inc.—For excerpts from David Mace, *Marriage, The Art of Lasting Love,* Copyright 1952.

Harper & Row Publishers—For excerpts from J. S. Bonnell, *Psychology for Pastor and People,* Copyright 1948.

Holt, Rinehart & Winston, Inc.—For excerpts from Erich Fromm, *Man for Himself,* Copyright 1947.

The Macmillan Co.—For excerpts from Phyllis McGinley, *Sixpence in Her Shoe,* Copyright 1964; and E. Kubler-Ross, *On Death and Dying,* Copyright 1969.

The Menninger Foundation—For permission to reproduce "The Criteria of Emotional Stability."

*Pastoral Psychology*—For excerpts from V. Kreyer, "Feelings of Handicapped Individuals" June 1965; and G.E. Bartlett, "The Minister: Pastor or Promoter" Sept. 1967.

Prentice-Hall, Inc.—For excerpts from D. Johnson, *Marriage Counseling: Theory and Practice,* Copyright 1961; and W. A. Clebsch and C. R. Jaekle, *Pastoral Care in Historical Perspective,* Copyright 1964.

# CONTENTS

# PREFACE

How do people handle their personal problems? According to a national survey that was conducted several years ago, many people do nothing except to hope that the situation will eventually take care of itself, others pray, and a sizable number turn to family and friends for counsel. When people decide to seek professional help, the survey found, 42 percent go to a clergyman, 29 percent see a physician, and the remainder go to a variety of other counselors, including psychologists and psychiatrists.[1]

While these figures may no longer be an accurate description of where people take their problems, there can be little doubt that many turn to the church in times of stress. Regardless of his training or desires, the church leader, and especially the pastor

> does not enjoy the privilege of electing whether or not he will counsel with...people. They inevitably bring their problems to him for his best guidance and wisest care. He cannot avoid this....His choice is not between counseling or not counseling, but between counseling in a disciplined and skilled way and counseling in an undisciplined and unskilled way.[2]

Counseling in a skilled way, however, is a very complex activity. Success depends first of all on a basic understanding of human behavior. In *Man in Transition*, volume 1 of the Psychology for Church Leaders Series, we attempted to broaden this understanding by discussing how normal individuals develop and handle the stresses of life. In volume 3 of the series, *Fractured Personalities*, we will consider what happens when the pressures get so great that people must resort to various kinds of abnormal behavior.

But skillful and successful counseling also involves knowledge of counseling techniques. It is to this issue that we turn in the following pages. Chapters 1 and 2 give an introduction to the practical "how to do it" of counseling. Then marital and vocational counseling are discussed, followed in chapter 5 by a consideration of counseling with the mentally and physically ill, the dying and bereaved, the physically handicapped, and the socially deprived. The last chapter gives some suggestions concerning ways to prevent problems from getting worse or from getting started in the first place.

When the report of the Joint Commission on Mental Health was sent to the United States Congress several years ago, it was noted that we have far too few psychologists, psychiatrists, social workers, and other highly trained counselors who can do all of the counseling that needs to be done. In the absence of professional personnel, the report concluded, "a host of persons untrained or partially trained in the mental health principles and practices" are working to help people with their problems.3 Church leaders are among this host. They are already involved in counseling although many could be doing a better job. As a step toward this end, the following chapters have been written.

Reading about counseling will never make one a counselor. Knowing what one is supposed to do and not do can be helpful, but skills are developed by getting involved. Some people get involved by plunging in on their own, but if there is a trained instructor around—such as a professor, an experienced pastor or a professional counselor—with whom you can discuss the ideas in this book and with whom you can evaluate your own counseling techniques, then the learning task will be faster and, hopefully, more efficient.

The people who helped with the first volume in this series have, in most cases, also been involved in the production of this second manuscript. Many of my colleagues at Trinity Evangelical Divinity School have made helpful suggestions about the following chapters and I am especially indebted to the assistance of Curtis Wennerdahl and John Hochevar. Mrs. Ronald Gifford typed the manuscript and my wife,

Julie, made many excellent comments and was a constant encouragement to me as I wrote. Finally, I want to thank the numerous pastors and other church leaders who, over the past few years, have shared some of their frustrations and difficulties in counseling with their people. This book has been written with the hope that it will bring help to these committed men and women.

GARY R. COLLINS

# 1
## *Basic Considerations in Counseling*

When the children of Israel were camped at the foot of Mount Horeb, Moses had a visit from his father-in-law, a man named Jethro (Ex. 18:1-7). The older man was glad to learn details about the journey from Egypt, but he was distressed to discover that Moses was spending entire days listening to complaints and "judging" the people. Then, as in-laws are sometimes inclined to do, Jethro decided to offer advice. He told Moses that he was wearing himself out and suggested that "able men" be selected to handle some of the less serious problems. These men were to be God-fearing, honest (Ex. 18:21), available "at all times" (18:22, RSV), and willing to refer the more difficult problems to Moses (18:26). Probably this counseling was mainly concerned with legal issues, but no doubt the counselors also dealt with personal problems. In this setting are seen some of the characteristics of effective counseling: a service performed by godly and capable people who are readily available for consultation and willing to refer the difficult cases to a more experienced person.[1]

Counseling can be defined as a relationship between two or more persons in which one person (the counselor) seeks to advise, encourage and/or assist another person or persons (the counselee[s]) to deal more effectively with the problems of life. Counseling may have any number of goals, including a changing of the counselee's behavior, attitudes or values;

preventing more serious problems from developing; teaching social skills; encouraging expression of emotions; giving support in times of need; instilling insight; guiding as a decision is made; teaching responsibility; stimulating spiritual growth; and helping the counselee to mobilize his inner resources in times of crisis. Unlike psychotherapy, counseling rarely aims to radically alter or remold the personality.

Because of his position, the church leader is in a unique counseling position. Unlike the professional, the pastoral counselor is often well acquainted with the counselee's personal, home and community background.* The church leader can visit in homes, he is often a trusted friend, and he is available—as near as the church or telephone. In addition, the pastoral counselor freely makes use of spiritual resources such as prayer and Bible reading. Since he strives to be an "expert in spiritual growth,"[2] the Christian counselor can be of special help to people who are concerned about God, values, sin, forgiveness, guilt, and other religious questions.

## THE SETTING FOR COUNSELING

Counseling can be done almost anywhere—in a home, in the pastor's office, in the parking lot, at the back of an empty church, or in a hospital room. Privacy is of importance, however, and for this reason it is best to find a quiet location where there will be a minimum of interruptions. Ringing telephones and people knocking at the door will hinder effective communication in counseling, and for this reason a do-not-disturb sign on the door, or someone who can answer the telephone, can often be a big help.

*The term "pastoral counseling" as used in this book refers to counseling that is done both by ordained clergymen and by laymen. Every believer is a priest (1 Pe. 2:5,9) who prays for others and bears the burdens of others (Gal. 6:2). In this sense every Christian is a pastoral counselor, even though we have not all been ordained for special service in the church.

14

There can be no hard and fast rules about the way in which a counseling room is furnished. Counseling can take place in a room that has four blank walls and two hard chairs, or in a more comfortable office that is attractively furnished with comfortable chairs, draperies, carpets, pictures and a couple of plants. If the church leader has an office where he does most of his counseling it is a good idea to sit in the counselee's chair for a few minutes and look around. Are you gazing into a bright light or facing a distracting picture? Is the chair comfortable? Do you have an unobstructed view of the counselor's chair? If the room is pleasantly furnished, the counselor and counselee are both likely to feel more relaxed and able to do a better job.

Arrangement of the furniture depends on the counselor's preference and on the size or shape of the office. No evidence suggests, for example, that counseling is more (or less) successful if the participants choose to sit on opposite sides of a desk or if they sit facing each other, although one study has shown that counselors and counselees both prefer *not* to have a desk between them.[3] The arrangement shown in Figure 1-1 allows the counselee his choice of a chair, and for the anxious person there is no need to feel that the counselor is sitting where he blocks the door.

Sometimes it is forgotten that the counselor's behavior also contributes to the setting. If he is busy leafing through papers, doodling, or slouching in his chair, he gives the impression that he is bored or more interested in other things. This was impressed on me in a particularly dramatic way at one time near the beginning of my counseling career. A young man with whom I had been counseling arrived for his appointment on time but found me on the telephone. When I finished my conversation I asked permission to make "one more call that can't wait." My counselee sat patiently until I had finished and then announced that I was obviously too busy to see him. "As a matter of fact," he volunteered, "I've got a lot to do myself." In spite of my attempts to reassure him, he left. For two weeks he didn't show for his scheduled appointment and when he did return it took another two or three interviews before we had restored the rapport that had previously existed. It is important, therefore, to convey the idea that we want to help as much as possible and that, at least for the present, there is nothing more important than the counselee and his problem.[4] Facial expressions, tone of voice, posture, and gestures all convey our real feelings. If we are sincerely interested in people and want to help, this will "come across" and will be one of our most valuable ways of getting the counseling off to a good start.

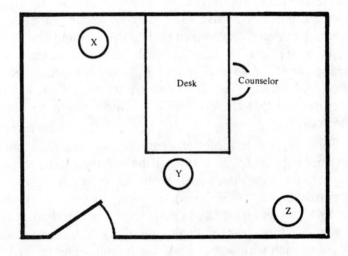

Figure 1-1

One way of arranging furniture in a counseling room. The counselee can sit in chair X, Y or Z.

# Personal Characteristics of the Counselor

## SELF-UNDERSTANDING

Freud believed that as a first step in becoming competent, the counselor must develop "insight into the...unconscious layers of his own soul."[5] To achieve this goal, he recommended that all counselors be analyzed by a trained therapist. While this suggestion has been rejected by most modern psychologists, it is generally agreed that self-understanding is a very desirable counselor characteristic. When we have unrecognized hostility, insecurity, unusual sexual urges, strong needs for acceptance, or other "hangups," these can come out in counseling and interfere with our ability to help others. If it is true, as R. May has suggested, that religious counselors tend to be highly ambitious, overly impressed with the importance of their work, inclined to condemn, and ill-at-ease in knowing how to handle their own sex urges, then we must guard against forcing these characteristics upon others.[6] By knowing about ourselves, we are better able to evaluate and control our own behavior, and we can more fully appreciate the feelings and actions of our counselees.[7] "The counselor who has not faced up to the problems of his own life, his own methods of evasion and self deception, his own rationalizations will have little understanding of these devices as they are employed by others."[8]

Self-knowledge includes an awareness of our beliefs and values. For many years it was believed that values never entered into counseling and that the counselor could maintain a position of complete neutrality in his interviews. We now know that this view was wrong. What we believe influences all of our interpersonal relations—including counseling—so we might as well recognize and accept our biases and, at times, even tell the counselee about them.[9] Once while working in the counseling center of a state university, a student appeared who was in the process of reevaluating his religious beliefs. He was especially critical of the denomination in which he was raised, which still held the allegiance of the rest of his family and which also happened to be the denomination to which I belonged. Instead of pretending otherwise, I told the student about my church membership and beliefs but encouraged him to continue with the expression of his negative feelings. We developed a warm counseling relationship and made real progress, even though we both knew that we did not agree on some basic values.

Self-knowledge can never be complete, but there are at least three ways in which we can come to know ourselves better. First is reflection on our own—taking a personal inventory of our characteristics, strengths and weaknesses. After looking conscientiously and honestly at ourselves, it is helpful to discuss the results with a respected friend or an experienced counselor. Frequently he will see things that we fail to recognize in ourselves. Third, there is the self-understanding that comes when we ask the Holy Spirit to guide the evaluation. The God of creation knows more about us than we will ever know (Ps. 139:1-6). With the psalmist we can pray, "Search me, O God, and know my heart: try me, and know my thoughts: and see if there be any wicked way in me, and lead me in the way everlasting" (Ps. 139:23-24).

## PSYCHOLOGICAL CHARACTERISTICS

Textbook writers have listed a number of psychological traits which are assumed to make counselors more effective, including sincerity, compassion, patience, flexibility, self-confidence, optimism, approachability, mental alertness, common sense, fairness, emotional stability, good grooming, freedom from distracting mannerisms, breadth of knowledge, and ability to keep from appearing shocked. While all are desirable and worth developing, it is unlikely that any one person could possess them all or that all are necessary for successful counseling. When effective counselors are compared with those who are less effective, it is evident that the most important counselor traits are understanding, acceptance, appropriate social distance, ability to get along with people, and experience. [10]

*Understanding of others.* If the relationship is to be fruitful, the counselor must have at least some understanding of the counselee. By listening carefully, watching the counselee's behavior during the interview, and attempting to see things from his perspective, we can increase our understanding of his feelings, attitudes and problems. In so doing, we also demonstrate our own interest and concern.

*Acceptance.* This involves genuine respect and interest in the counselee as a "person" rather than as a "case." Such acceptance does not necessarily mean approval or agreement, for we may not like a person's opinions and may conclude that his past behavior is repulsive or sinful. But we must accept him as a person whom God loves and for whom Christ died.

Some people are always more likable and easier to accept than others. By developing an ability and willingness to tolerate individual differences, we can learn to accept those who are not innately attractive. The Holy Spirit can also help us to accept those who are unlovely, since God Himself has shown that He is concerned about people who are unattractive sinners (Ro. 5:8).

*Social distance.* Counselors were once taught that they should be completely uninvolved and emotionally detached from their counselees, but today it is recognized that cold aloofness and close personal involvement are equally undesirable. The counselor must be enough detached so that he can be objective but enough involved so that he can "feel with" the counselee, and occasionally express his own emotions or share something from his personal experience.

*Ability to get along with people.* Good counselors are at ease in a variety of social settings. If a person has trouble relating to people in general, this will not suddenly change in a counseling room. The key to success is "not so much the techniques employed, important as they are, as it is the total attitude of the counselor, how he feels about people, what he believes about them and about himself."[11]

This does not mean that we will approach all counseling sessions with complete ease and self-confidence. Often, especially at the beginning, counselors feel anxious as they approach an interview. When the counselee walks through the door expecting us to help with a personal problem, all our textbook knowledge suddenly seems to vanish and we sometimes feel very inadequate. Often these feelings disappear as the interview progresses, and they become less intense with further training and more experience.

*Experience.* Counselors with greater experience often show more self-confidence and an increased ability to understand, accept, and successfully help their counselees.[12]

## SPIRITUAL CHARACTERISTICS

The effective Christian counselor must also possess spiritual qualifications. First he must be a Christian, having personally experienced the new birth (Jn. 3:3) by believing that the risen Christ is the Son of God (Jn. 3:15-17; Ro. 10:9). Then, as in the days of Moses, pastoral counselors should be capable, God-fearing, honest, readily available, and willing to get help when they encounter difficult cases (Ex. 18:21-22). The counselor should also be a student who is thoroughly familiar with the Word of God (2 Ti. 2:15), and a man who seeks to be a follower of Christ (1 Pe. 2:21) whose very name is "Wonderful Counselor" (Is. 9:6, RSV).

## CHARACTERISTICS OF THE COUNSELEE

Effective counseling is not completely dependent on the counselor's characteristics and skills. If the counselee is uncooperative or uninterested in changing his behavior, the interviews will not be very fruitful, regardless of the counselor's skills. When children are forced to "talk with the pastor," for example, or when rebellious delinquents are *sent* for psychiatric help, often there is little improvement. For best results, the counselee must really want to change. He should have a favorable opinion of the counselor and of counseling, an expectation that things will get better, and a willingness to face himself in the work of honest introspection. If he is lacking these characteristics, try to discuss his feelings and attitudes before attempting to counsel him.

## COUNSELING SKILLS AND TECHNIQUES

Good counseling is difficult work. It is time-consuming, emotionally draining, physically exhausting and frequently unsuccessful. By developing proficiency in the following skills and techniques, however, we should be able to increase our overall counseling effectiveness.

### BEFORE THE INTERVIEW

Whenever possible, it is best to spend a few minutes in preparation prior to the start of a counseling session. When we receive guests into our homes, we usually tidy the house and give the appearance that the guest is welcome and expected. A person coming for counseling should be received with at least as much courtesy. If he feels that he is "taking the valuable time of a busy man" he may feel guilty, rushed, and hence unable to communicate. It is a good procedure, therefore, to straighten the papers on the desk, get the room in readiness, and arrange to keep the counseling period free from interruptions.

Then we should review the counselee's case history and remind ourselves of the details of any previous counseling with him. It is embarrassing to get one person's problem confused with another's, and it is distressing to the counselee, who naturally prefers to think that he and his problems are uppermost in your mind.

For the Christian counselor it is also important to prepare for the interview with prayer. We can commit the counseling session to God, asking that we will be made sensitive to the needs and feelings of the counselee, and that we will be led by the Holy Spirit as we counsel.[13] Such prayer is no substitute for training and preparation, but all our activities, including those for which we are highly trained, should be committed to the Lord who guides our thoughts and actions (Pr. 16:3; 3:5-6). The counselor should meet the counselee at the exact time of the appointment. Being ten or fifteen minutes late and giving no real explanation will make the counselee assume he has been forgotten or that he isn't important enough to meet on time.

## DURING THE INTERVIEW

When we meet somebody in a social situation, we do not usually engage in frantic activity to remember all the social graces our parents taught us. If the home training was adequate, the social skills appear automatically. To some extent, the same is true of counseling, for we do not "pull out a bag of tricks" as soon as a counselee enters the office. If we are aware of the following skills and think about them frequently as we prepare for counseling, many will appear automatically when we are face to face with the counselee. This does not mean that the counselor should not think about techniques during the interview. He should be asking himself constantly, "What is happening now?" "What am I doing?" "What is best to do next?" But the counseling session must be primarily a relationship between concerned people rather than a period during which the counselor is so concerned about skills that he forgets everything else.

*Start by working on the relationship.* Counselees often approach an interview with fear, trembling, and a number of misconceptions. They may be uncomfortable at the thought of discussing their personal problems and uncertain about what is going to happen during the interview. At the

22

beginning, therefore, the counselor has a responsibility to support and stimulate the counselee.[14] *Support* involves "breaking the ice" with a casual comment or two and inviting the counselee to have a seat. With some counselees it might be desirable to give an indication of what will happen during the interview. For example, the counselor might say, "I'm glad for this opportunity to chat about the things that are concerning you." This is much less threatening than an emotionally loaded statement like "I'm glad for this chance to counsel you about your problems."

When someone brings a problem to a psychologist, the initial contact is usually a meeting between two strangers; but in pastoral counseling, the counselor and counselee often know each other at least casually. If the counselor is a minister, he has been observed in the pulpit or met as he shakes hands at the door following the service. The Sunday school teacher or youth leader who is asked for counsel has probably demonstrated his warmth and concern for people in noncounseling situations such as Bible-study classes. These casual precounseling experiences do a great deal to establish a relationship long before the counselee ever knocks at your door.

In addition to giving support and helping the person feel more at ease, we must *stimulate* him to talk. For some counselees this is no problem because they talk freely when given the chance. But, for others, talking is difficult, even if they have requested an appointment and really want to discuss some problem. If the counselee has come voluntarily a comment such as "What would you like to talk about today?" or "Now, you wanted to talk to me?" can get things started. Very often the counselee will respond by saying, "I just don't know where to start." At such times it might be good to show understanding: "Probably a lot of things all tie in together," and then to encourage the person: "Start anyplace and eventually we will get the whole picture," or "Begin where it seems easiest." These statements, of course, are merely examples of any number of appropriate comments.

Occasionally a person wants to talk about some problem but is reluctant to mention it. Every college counseling center has students who come requesting information for a term paper that they are writing on homosexuality, masturbation, or some similar topic; or they request help for a "friend" who has some problem. While these may be the real reasons for their coming, at times the "paper" or "friend" is a cover which enables the counselee to size up a counselor who, he hopes, will give him an opportunity to discuss his own homosexual tendencies, masturbation problems, or other concerns. A tactful suggestion that the problem may be personal will sometimes bring denials, but often this will give the counselee the encouragement he needs to start talking.

Sometimes a church leader may take the initiative by approaching a person who appears to need counseling. In such cases it is a good idea to get to your point as soon as possible. "I have missed you in church for the past several Sundays" or "I wanted to chat with you about the youth group" lets the counselee know right at the start why the interview has been requested.

*Listen attentively.* Church leaders spend a lot of their time talking. This, after all, is an important part of their job, but too often it carries over into interviews as the counselor feels that he must be constantly giving sage advice or asking a lot of questions. Such an attitude greatly hinders good counseling.

> Just as love to God begins with listening to His Word, so the beginning of love for the brethren is learning to listen to them....Many people are looking for an ear that will listen. They do not find it among Christians, because these Christians are talking when they should be listening. But he who can no longer listen to his brother will soon be no longer listening

24

to God either; he will be doing nothing but prattle in the presence of God too....One who cannot listen long and patiently will presently be talking beside the point and be never really speaking to others, albeit he be not conscious of it. [15]

When we learn to listen, the counselee has the opportunity to express his feelings, "let off steam," or "get things off his chest." In so doing, he often feels better, and at the same time gives us valuable information that we might have missed otherwise.

Listening is not a passive activity; it is an art which requires alert concentration and undivided attention. It has been estimated that we speak about 125 words per minute, but that our thinking is four times that fast. [16] Therefore, it is possible to listen to a speaker and still be able to think about other things. In a counseling session we must be careful not to let our minds wander, especially when we are bored. Instead, we must listen to what is being said, try not to show disapproval or shock, and attempt to understand things from the speaker's point of view. An occasional head nod, smile, "uh-huh," or general type of question (such as "What then?" "How did you feel about that?" or "Anything else?") can keep the counselee talking.

*Watch carefully.* A good counselor can learn a great deal by carefully observing the counselee's speech and actions. Suppose, for example, that there are changes in voice pitch and volume or shifts in the topic of conversation. If we review what was said both before and after these changes, we may detect a topic which is of special importance or concern to the counselee. Sometimes we see inconsistencies or gaps in a story. The person who says he is happy in his work but later talks about changing jobs, or the person who describes his family but forgets to mention his father, may be revealing something that we might ask about later.

The opening statement can also be revealing. "My mother

sent me" gives a clue that the counselee may be somewhat less than enthusiastic about talking with a counselor. Likewise, the closing remarks often give an indication of the counselee's view of what happened. Finally, we should watch for repeated references to the same topic, for this may give a clue to what is uppermost on the person's mind.[17]

There is an old saying that "actions speak louder than words," and this is true in many counseling situations. Tears or near tears, fighting, shifts in posture, or changes in breathing can all be clues that the person is dealing with important emotional issues. If a student changes his position and gets a little misty-eyed when talking about grades, this may be a subject about which he is especially concerned. Sometimes it is a good idea to make a mental note about your observation and at a later time bring the topic up again. If the tears return, this is a clue that here is a potential problem, even though the student may not have identified it as such.

At this point someone may ask, "Why do all this detective work? Why don't we just deal with the guy's problem?" This would be ideal if every counselee first had an understanding of what his real problem was and, second, if every counselee were willing and able to share his problem. Very frequently, however, neither of these conditions exists. When a patient has a recurring pain, the doctor doesn't prescribe more pain pills and go on to the next patient. Instead, the physician tries to discover and treat the cause of the pain. Similarly, the counselor and counselee must work together to reach the underlying cause of the problem. When this is not clearly apparent, the counselor must be alert to the more subtle clues that the counselee is giving (usually unconsciously).

*Don't be afraid of silence.* When nothing is being said, most of us feel very uncomfortable; but in counseling such silence is often very meaningful. It may indicate that the counselee is struggling to control an emotion, thinking

26

about an important issue, or debating whether to tell you more. At such times an understanding comment like "It's hard to talk sometimes, isn't it?" or an encouraging remark such as "Take your time" can let the counselee know that it is all right to be silent. The counselor can then keep quiet for a while until his counselee is ready to share more of his ideas and feelings.

*Question wisely.* Beginning counselors often make the mistake of asking too many questions. Once you start this, the counselee draws two kinds of conclusions. First, he concludes that counseling is simply the answering of questions that are asked by the counselor. Second, he expects that once the counselor has asked all of his questions and obtained the answers, then he will give his solution to the problem. This puts the counselor in a very awkward situation. Usually he doesn't have a "pat" solution, and sometimes he becomes so busy thinking up new questions to ask that he has no time to listen to the counselee's answers.

It is best to use questions sparingly and to think before you ask. Use the following guidelines:

1. Ask open-ended questions. An open-ended question is very broad and gives the counselee plenty of opportunity to respond with his opinions or further information. "How did you feel about failing?" or "What do you think now about your religious training?" or "What happened next?" are broad questions which stimulate further discussion. In contrast, "closed" questions like "Were you frustrated because you failed?" "Do you think your religious training was not relevant?" or "Is that the end of your story?" invite a one-word answer like "yes." Then the counselor feels inclined to ask another question.

2. Avoid either-or questions. "Do you want to get married or stay single?" presents two alternatives. The counselee responds with his preference and the discussion stops.

3. Try to use indirect questions. Direct questions are

27

straight queries; indirect questions inquire without seeming to do so. "How does it feel to have your marriage breaking up?" is direct. "I wonder how it feels to have your marriage breaking up" is indirect. Both of these require an answer and both show the counselor's interest, but the indirect question keeps the counselee from feeling that he is being quizzed.[18]

4. Avoid a series of questions. I once appeared on a radio program in which the interviewer questioned me somewhat as follows. "Do Christians ever crack up? By this I mean do people in the church show more neurotic symptoms than the unchurched, and does the church have anything to do with mental illness and treatment?" When I heard a barrage of questions like that, I never knew which question to answer first. Such questioning is frustrating to the counselee and often brings forth a remarkably small amount of useful information.

5. Ask "Why?" sparingly. This question can sometimes provide us with helpful information ("Why did you decide to become a Christian?"), but often it has a negative, rejecting connotation ("Why were you late for your appointment?").

It is probably true that "no more effective method has ever been devised for helping people reach the goals of self-knowledge and personal integration than through a profound understanding of the technique of asking questions." [19] Jesus used questions skillfully, and the pastoral counselor would be wise to do the same.

*Learn how to respond.* Porter has suggested that there are five commonly used counselor responses: evaluative, interpretative, supportive, probing, and understanding.[20] *Probing* responses are used when more information is needed or when the counselor wants to stimulate further discussion. With *understanding* responses, the counselor wants to convey his comprehension and empathy. By using *supportive* comments, the counselor tries to reassure or encourage the counselee. *Interpretative* responses are meant to teach the counselee or show him what is happening, while *evaluative* responses indicate what the counselor thinks about the goodness, rightness or wisdom of an action or idea. To this we might add *action* responses in which the counselor tries to encourage or stimulate the counselee to engage in some kind of action. Examples of each of these kinds of responses are shown in Table 1-1.

Although it tends to be overused by some pastoral counselors, the *reflective* type of comment is also appropriate at times. Here the counselor tries to reflect the counselee's feelings by repeating or slightly rephrasing the counselee's statements. Such responses indicate that we understand feelings and are encouraging further conversation. The following is an example:

Counselee: Pastor, I've wanted to talk about my problem for a long time, but couldn't bring myself to come here.

Counselor: It's been hard to talk?

Counselee: Yes, but I have to talk to someone, so I'm going to tell you the whole story. I've prayed about this but I don't understand why God seems far away.

Counselor: God seems far away at times?

Counselee: Yes, but even so, I have been trusting Him to help with my problem.

Counselor: You keep on trusting, even though God seems far away.

In counseling, all types of responses should be used at times, although one or two may predominate in any given interview. In addition to these verbal responses, such things

## Table 1-1

### Types of Counselor Responses

| | |
|---|---|
| Probing | Tell me more about this.<br>How does your wife feel about it?<br>What then?<br>Uh-huh.<br>I'm not sure I understand. |
| Understanding | This must be very hard.<br>In other words, you feel....<br>So far, you've said....<br>I see.<br>These are very trying times for you. |
| Supportive | Many people feel this way.<br>I'm sure they will understand.<br>Things will get better when.... |
| Interpretive | What seems to be happening is....<br>This makes you feel guilty.<br>You're very dependent on....<br>You seem to be saying that.... |
| Evaluative | That was wise.<br>This is a good start.<br>The Bible says that is sin.<br>That's not likely to work.<br>I suspect you'll want to change that. |
| Action | I would advise you to....<br>Why don't you....<br>Before you come back next week....<br>You shouldn't.... |

as head nods, approving looks and smiles, or even periods of silence can stimulate further discussion or convey to the counselee how we are reacting.

Sometimes the counselee will ask a direct question. Many of these seem to be legitimate requests for information, while at other times people ask questions because this is their way of initiating conversation (e.g., "What do you think of the weather today?"). Sometimes questions have hidden meanings. For example, "Where did you go to school?" may be an expression of curiosity about the counselor but it could also be a concern about his competence. "Where did you get your drapes?" or similar questions in the middle of an interview may be an attempt by the counselee to change the subject. How we respond to questions will depend somewhat on what is being asked. Usually a straightforward answer is desirable, but in all cases the counselor should be sensitive to the counselee's possible reasons for asking the question when he does.

*Make use of spiritual resources.* Two of the greatest weaknesses of pastoral counselors are an over and under use of spiritual resources. Some Christians are of the opinion that reading the Bible or saying a prayer is all that is needed for successful counseling. Sometimes this *is* all that is needed, but in most cases such an approach is likely to be unsuccessful and frustrating to the counselee. It also gives the impression that Bible reading and prayer are magic charms that suddenly make everything right. At the other extreme are pastoral counselors who tend to ignore prayer and the Scriptures in their counseling, using psychological techniques almost exclusively.

Once again, no hard and fast rules can be given for the use of prayer or Bible reading. Many Christian counselors pray aloud at the beginning and/or end of an interview, and sometimes they "feel led" to pray at other times. Paul Tournier, the famous Swiss counselor, likes to have a period of "quiet communion" during which both parties silently acknowledge the presence and influence of God.[21] When it seems relevant, the counselor may also want to read a Bible passage during an interview. Narramore feels this makes more of an impression if the Bible is handed to the counselee and he is asked to read the indicated portion.[22] For this, a modern-language version may be especially helpful and, whatever the translation, it is usually wise to discuss the meaning of a passage after it is read. Table 1-2 lists a number of helpful scriptural references. Christian counselees should also be encouraged to spend daily time in Bible reading, prayer, and quiet meditation. It is also helpful to suggest devotional reading at times, or—when consistent with one's denominational practices—to even have a small communion service.

The extent to which spiritual resources will be used in counseling depends on the counselor, the counselee, and the problem. The Christian counselor should pray both during a personal daily time of devotions and during the day as he goes about his activities. Certainly the counselor who never prays in private will be awkward and uncomfortable if he prays in an interview. In like manner, the Christian should be thoroughly familiar with the Word of God (2 Ti. 2:15), or he won't have much success using the Bible in an interview.

For some counselees, prayer and Scripture reading during an interview will be a strengthening and reassuring experience. For others, this would be a source of considerable embarrassment and discomfort. Therefore, the counselor must use careful judgment in deciding if, when, and how he introduces such practices. To some extent, this will be dictated by the counselee's problem. The grief-stricken widow could be greatly comforted by a dependence on such spiritual resources, whereas the college student who is in danger of flunking out of school might prefer to have a short prayer followed by a long discussion of his study habits.

# Table 1-2
# Helpful Scripture References for Use in Counseling

| Need or problem | Scripture References |
|---|---|
| Anxiety and worry | Ps. 43:5; 46:1-2, 9-11; Pr. 3:5-6; Mt. 6:31-32; Phil. 4:6-7, 19; 1 Pe. 5:6-7. |
| Anger | Ps. 37:8; Ja. 1:19; Col. 3:8. |
| Comfort | Ps. 23:4; Lam. 3:22-23; Mt. 5:4; 11:28-30; Jn. 14:16, 18; Ro. 8:28; 2 Co. 1:3-4; 2 Th. 2:16-17. |
| Courage | Jos. 1:7-9; Ps. 27:3; 31:24; Pr. 3:26; 14:26; Mt. 28:20; 2 Co. 5:6; Eph. 3:11-17; Phil. 4:13; 2 Ti. 1:8-9. |
| Death (facing) | Ps. 23:4; 116:15; Jn. 14:1-6; Ro. 14:8; 1 Th. 5:9-10; 2 Ti. 4:7-8; Rev. 21:4. |
| Discouragement | Jos. 1:9; Ps. 27:14; 34:4-8, 17-19; 43:5; 55:22; Mt. 11:28-30; Jn. 14:1, 27; 16:33; 2 Co. 4:8-9; Heb. 4:16. |
| Doubts | Ps. 37:5; Pr. 3:5-6; Jn. 7:17; 20:24-30; Heb. 11:6. |
| Envy | Ps. 37:1-7; Pr. 23:17; Ro. 13:13; Gal. 5:26. |
| Faith | Ro. 4:3; 10:17; Eph. 2:8-9; Heb. 11:6; Ja. 1:3. |
| Fear | Ps. 27:1, 8, 14; 46:1-2; 56:11; Is. 43:1-5; 51:12; Jn. 14:27; Ro. 8:31; 1 Jn. 4:18. |
| Forgiveness for sin | Ps. 32:5; 51:1-19; Pr. 28:13; Is. 55:7; 1 Jn. 1:9; Ja. 5:15-16. |
| Forgiving others | Mt. 5:44; 6:14; Mk. 11:25; Lk. 17:3-4; Eph. 4:32; Col. 3:13. |
| Grief and sorrow | Ps. 23:4; Mt. 5:4; 11:28-30; Jn. 14:16, 18; 16:22; Phil. 1:21; 1 Th. 4:13; 2 Th. 2:16-17; Rev. 21:4. |
| Guidance | Ps. 32:8; Pr. 3:5-6; Jn. 16:13. |
| Hatred | Eph. 4:31-32; 1 Jn. 1:9; 2:9-11. |
| Helplessness | Ps. 34:7; 37:5, 24; 55:22; 91:4; Heb. 4:16; 13:5-6; 1 Pe. 5:7. |
| Loneliness | Ps. 27:10; Pr. 18:24; Jn. 15:14; Heb. 13:5. |
| Needs | Ps. 34:10; 37:3-4; 84:11; Phil. 4:19. |
| Patience | Heb. 10:36; Gal. 5:22 (long-suffering); Ja. 1:3-4; 5:7-8, 11. |
| Peace of mind | Is. 26:3; Jn. 14:27; 16:33; Ro. 5:1; Phil. 4:7; Col. 3:15. |
| Praise | Ps. 34:1; 50:23; 107:8; 139:14; Heb. 13:15. |
| Problems and trials | Mt. 5:10-11; Ro. 8:28; 2 Co. 4:17; 2 Ti. 3:12; Heb. 12:7, 11; 1 Pe. 2:20; Rev. 3:19. |
| Salvation | Ro. 3:10, 23; 10:9; 1 Jn. 1:9-10; Jn. 3:16; 5:24; 10:10; Lk. 19:10; Ac. 4:12; Ro. 6:23; Eph. 2:8-9. |
| Sickness | Ps. 103:3; Ja. 5:14-15. |
| Sin | Ps. 51:1-4, 10-12; Is. 53:5-6; 55:7; 59:1-2; Ro. 3:23; 6:23; 1 Jn. 1:9. |
| Spiritual growth | 2 Ti. 2:15; 2 Pe. 1:5-8; 3:13-14. |
| Temptation | 1 Co. 10:12-13; Heb. 2:18; Ja. 1:2-4, 12; 2 Pe. 2:9. |
| Unhappiness | Jn. 15:10-12; Gal. 5:22. |
| Weakness | Ps. 27:14; 28:7; Is. 40:29, 31; 41:10; 2 Co. 12:9; Phil. 4:13. |
| Wisdom and understanding | Pr. 4:7; Job 28:23; Ja. 1:5. |

*End positively*. It is desirable to end an interview smoothly and, when possible, to have the counselee go away with feelings of hope and encouragement. But occasionally this is difficult and counselors are sometimes at a loss to know how a counseling session should be stopped.

If things are moving smoothly, it is wise to give the counselee a hint that the end is near. By keeping a clock on the desk or on a distant wall it is possible to keep track of the time without having to keep glancing at your watch. A statement like "Our time is just about up" gives the counselee a warning but indicates that there is still time to pick up loose ends. In the remaining minutes it may be helpful to summarize what has happened during the interview, or discuss what the counselee should do next. Sometimes a word of encouragement or a short prayer is appropriate.

Occasionally counselees will bring up significant new material during these last few minutes of the interview. This may be an attempt to prolong the interview or it may indicate an unconscious desire to raise issues at a "safe" time when it is not possible to discuss the matter further. At such times a comment like "That would be a good topic for us to discuss next time" prevents the interview from continuing and gives a good opener for your next counseling session.

AFTER THE INTERVIEW

When the counselee leaves, the counselor should jot down some notes and briefly evaluate the interview. This should be done immediately so that details are not forgotten. When your reactions and a summary of the session are recorded on paper, you have a convenient "memory jogger" to consult before the next interview.

The counselor must keep the interview in his confidence. Some pastors are sincerely amazed that even though their availability is well advertised still nobody comes for counseling. Frequently these are the men who like to describe counseling cases in sermons or who let counseling details slip into other casual conversations. Even when the names and details are changed, counselees and prospective counselees often decide to go for counseling to a person who will keep quiet. At times, of course, the counselor may wish to discuss the situation with a more experienced counselor for helpful suggestions, but these confidants should be few and selected with extreme care. If a pastor's wife cannot keep quiet, for example, she cannot expect to know anything about her husband's counseling ministry.

## OTHER CONSIDERATIONS

*Appointments.* At times a Christian counselor is needed immediately and without warning. When a loved one dies or a person suddenly becomes ill, the pastor must be available to offer whatever help or support he can.

For most other counseling, however, it is best to set a specific prearranged appointment. This is more convenient for everyone involved. The counselee knows his problem is being taken seriously and that a block of time is being reserved specifically for him, and the counselor is better able to budget his time for his other responsibilities.[23]

Professional counselors limit the length of an interview to fifty minutes. There is nothing sacred about this, but many experienced counselors feel that when a session is longer, less is accomplished. We are probably most efficient when we limit counseling sessions to between thirty and sixty minutes. Often this can be stated at the time of making the appointment: "Let's get together for an hour or so on Tuesday at three."

Every religious counselor will at some time encounter the person who feels free to call frequently at all hours of the day or night, and often at meal times. These people have needs, but the counselor also has some privileges and rights to privacy with his family. The frequent caller must at times be told politely and firmly, "I have some other responsibilities right now, so let's discuss this at our next session together."

*Keeping records.* Counselors frequently keep three kinds of records: notes during the interview, tape recordings, and notes recorded after the counselee has left. These records are helpful in providing the counselor with a review prior to the next counseling session, in helping him to evaluate his own progress and development, and in showing the counselee at a later time how he has changed.

Counselors differ in the extent to which they become involved with note-taking during an interview. Some avoid the practice; others take copious notes. There is a danger of getting so involved in taking notes, however, that we miss a lot of what the counselee is communicating. If he wants to take notes, the counselor might make a matter-of-fact comment at the start of the interview, such as, "I'd like to jot down a few things as we talk, so I can keep the whole picture in mind." Then, during the interview he should limit his writing to brief statements which can be elaborated later. He should also avoid writing anything that he is not prepared to have the counselee see. An interviewer was once called out of his office during an interview. When he returned, the counselee said, "I saw what you wrote about me being hostile and uncooperative!"[24] Such evaluative comments are best written into a summary notation after the counselee has left.

Tape recordings of counseling sessions can be very revealing. It takes a long time to listen to the recording, but in so doing the counselor can detect many of his own poor techniques that he might not recognize otherwise. At times it is also helpful to a counselee if he can hear tapes of earlier counseling sessions. Tape recordings should never be made in secret without the counselee's prior permission. This permission is not hard to get if the counselor explains his purpose in recording and assures the counselee that the tape will be kept confidential. Then it is probably best to set the recorder up where it can be seen. After a few self-conscious minutes, both counselee and counselor usually relax and forget that the recorder is operating.

Tapes, along with notes taken during and after an interview, should be kept in a locked cabinet. If this is not possible, it is probably best that records not be kept at all.

*Psychological tests.* Psychologists and school counselors often make use of psychological tests which measure intelligence, interests, special abilities, or personality. Some of these tests give results which could be helpful to a pastoral counselor, but the administration and interpretation of such tests are usually time-consuming, skillful tasks. Since relatively few church leaders have the professional skills or available time to use these instruments, it is best to have the testing done by a school counselor or qualified psychologist. This does not rule out the use of questionnaires and short "inventories" that are designed for use in pastoral counseling and are especially helpful in giving background information about a counselee. Like notes and other records, test results should be kept confidential and locked in a safe place.

## COUNSELING ETHICS

Every counselor, whether professional or nonprofessional, should be concerned about his ethical responsibilities and obligations. As Christians, we are responsible to God, the counselee and the community for what we do in a counseling situation. If a counselee informs us that he plans to commit murder, for example, we have an obligation to interfere in a way that will protect the counselee and his proposed victim. Many ethical decisions are not that clear-cut, however, and at times we must search the Scriptures and seek for the guidance of the Holy Spirit as we decide what to do in a given situation.

The following broad guidelines are basic "musts" for any pastoral counselor:

*Keep confidences.* What is told in confidence should be kept in confidence. This means that information should not be shared without the counselee's permission, and that material from interviews should generally not be presented as sermon illustrations. The good counselor also avoids discussing one counselee and his problem with another counselee.

*Avoid physical contact.* Apart from a handshake, it is usually best to avoid touching a counselee. Sometimes sexual and other emotional involvement begins—at least in the counselee's mind—when physical contact is permitted.

*Do not use counselees to satisfy your own desires.* The counselor's own curiosity, sexual desires, or need for people to be dependent on him, often influences his counseling. It may be interesting to hear the counselee tell you some gossip, but this is not beneficial if it merely satisfies your curiosity. An understanding of one's own weak points as well as reliance on the Holy Spirit help the counselor to avoid such temptations.

*Do not try to hide your Christian values.* The counselor's beliefs will enter everything he does, including his counseling. It is only fair to the counselee, therefore, that he have some knowledge of his counselor's Christian commitment. To do otherwise is a form of dishonesty.

*Do not force or pressure the counselee to continue counseling.* We can encourage people to get counseling, but the person who does not want help will probably not change—regardless of the counselor.

*Recognize your limitations.* Apart from Jesus, no one counselor ever has the ability and training to help everyone who needs or wants help. Some people should be referred to a more experienced counselor, or to a lawyer, medical doctor, or other specialist. "It is a sign of maturity when a counselor knows that he is not capable of making all of the necessary diagnoses and is willing to refer a counselee to one who may be better able to meet his particular needs. This attitude will add stature to the counselor and people will respect him for it."[25]

## DANGERS IN COUNSELING

When an ocean liner approaches port, a pilot will often come aboard to guide the ship to the pier. Because he has special knowledge of the rocks and shallow places, the pilot is able to take the ship around these danger points and prevent it from running aground.

In counseling, there are also a number of hidden dangers. When we are aware of them, we are less likely to run into difficulties that might otherwise seriously hinder our counseling effectiveness. Some of the more common dangers in counseling include the following.

### OVERRELIANCE ON ONE-SIDED INFORMATION

All of us describe events and problems *as we see them* from our own perspective. In counseling, we usually hear only one side of an issue—the counselee's—but this may be only part of the story. In some situations, such as in marriage and family counseling, we should try to get the views of other involved or knowledgeable people. Sometimes it is amazing to see how differently a husband and wife view a crumbling marriage. If the counselor relies on one account only, he is in danger of receiving a distorted view of the problem, taking sides, losing objectivity, or reducing his potential effectiveness as a counselor.

### JUMPING TO PREMATURE CONCLUSIONS

The counselor must listen attentively and avoid making early conclusions about a problem and its solutions. By trying to move too quickly, we may waste a lot of time and mental energy, since the problem which the counselee describes at first may not be the real or most pressing problem.

## OVERINVOLVEMENT

It is difficult for compassionate and sensitive people to be objective in their counseling. Too often we are tempted to shoulder the problems of other people and to get overly involved emotionally. Motives for this may be noble, but such overinvolvement is emotionally and physically wearing. It interferes with our family relationships and hinders our effectiveness in dealing with noncounseling responsibilities. We must bear one another's burdens (Gal. 6:2), and it would be wrong to forget about the counselee as soon as he walks out of the door, but for the sake of our health, our family, our overall efficiency, and our future counseling effectiveness, we must remain somewhat detached and objective.

Some counselees manipulate by making excessive and incessant demands. Forgetting about the counselor's private life or other responsibilities, they will try to rob him of his privacy and expect immediate attention whenever they call. With such people, we must set clear limits. A kind but strong comment like "I'm sorry Mrs. Smith, but right now I'm tied up. Let's discuss it after the prayer meeting tomorrow evening" is a tactful way of saying "Not now!"

## CLOSE ASSOCIATIONS WITH THE OPPOSITE SEX

Just because a counselor is a Christian there is no guarantee he will never be stimulated by members of the opposite sex (or, in some cases, by members of the same sex). In the one-to-one intimacy of an interview, some counselees are seductive and overly attracted to the counselor, and it can also work the other way!

> One of the counselor's hardest tasks is to keep the counselee from becoming attached to him or her; and if the readiness for emotional attachment is present on the counselor's side too, the counseling relationship is irreparably ruined. Whenever the counselor finds himself taking subjective pleasure in the presence of the counselee's person, he had better be wary.[26]

Occasionally following an interview a counselee will

40

charge that the counselor made physical advances. Such allegations are difficult to disprove because it is the counselor's word against the counselee's. At times like these it is important to have a good reputation! Techniques such as keeping the door slightly ajar as you counsel or having other people in the building can be a safeguard against such problems. In addition, many pastors and youth workers avoid counseling in cars, do not meet their counselees in secluded places, and refrain from calling on strangers unless accompanied by a deacon or other church worker.

### INFORMATION SLIPS

In spite of the counselor's best intentions, there is always a danger that he will inadvertently reveal some confidential information. To avoid this, we should make it a practice not to talk about other people (Ja. 3:1-10; 1 Pe. 3:10). As already emphasized, confidential material should never be used in public addresses, and information should not be given over the phone.

### FAILURE TO REFER

Some problems are too difficult and time-consuming for the religious counselor to handle alone. People with deep-seated emotional problems, suicidal tendencies and destructive urges should be referred to a professional counselor, but sometimes it is difficult to determine how this should be done. The problem of referral is considered in more detail in the next chapter.

### OVER- OR UNDER-EMPHASIS ON THE SPIRITUAL

Earlier in the chapter over- and under-emphasis on the spiritual were suggested as the two greatest weaknesses of pastoral counselors. To assume that all problems are best dealt with by prayer and Bible reading is as naïve and inefficient as the assumption that there is no place for God in the counseling interview. The pastoral counselor is in a unique position both to apply psychological counseling skills and to deal with relevant spiritual matters.

## A LOPSIDED MINISTRY

Sometimes the minister or other religious worker so enjoys his counseling that he begins to neglect his other responsibilities. He forgets that he is called and trained to be something other than a psychologist. He fails to realize that people who imitate "doctors, lawyers, psychiatrists, counselors, and social workers...frequently become merely incompetent amateurs or inexpert apprentices in acts properly belonging to others."[27]

Counseling is an important part of the ministry, and the church leader should strive to be as effective a counselor as possible. But he must remember that, unless he is involved in a specialized counseling ministry, he also has responsibility for the preparation of addresses and other leadership tasks in the church. Sometimes because of an overemphasis on counseling, private prayer is all but eliminated and there is increasingly less time for study. The church leader must guard against this. Some of his interviews may have to be shortened, and at times it may be necessary to limit the number of available hours for counseling. Otherwise he will develop a lopsided and generally less effective ministry.

## SUMMARY

Counseling is a relationship between at least two persons, one of whom (the counselor) seeks to advise, encourage, and/or assist another person (the counselee) to more effectively deal with the problems of life. Whether he is prepared for this or not, the church leader is likely to be involved in counseling as an important part of his work.

Effective counseling requires that we be alert to details of the setting in which counseling takes place, to the personal characteristics and attitudes of the participants, and to the skills and techniques of the counselor. Whenever possible, the counselor should get ready for the interview prior to the counselee's arrival. When the interview begins, the counselor should strive to build a good relationship with the counselee, listen attentively, watch carefully, make use of silent periods, question wisely, respond appropriately to the counselee's remarks, and make periodic use of such spiritual resources as prayer and Bible reading. After the interview it is wise to spend a few minutes evaluating what happened in the counseling session and making a few notes to refresh your memory in the future.

There are ethics and potential dangers in counseling, just as in any other professional activity. An awareness of these ethical considerations and dangers will contribute to the overall effectiveness of the counselor's activities.

Every counseling problem is not handled in the same way. Sometimes people need encouragement, sometimes they need advice, and at times they really need someone to listen while they pour out their troubles. The different types of counseling are considered in the next chapter.

## 2
# The Course of Counseling

Even when they have a knowledge of counseling techniques, pastoral counselors experience "deep feelings of frustration, uncertainty, and even a sense of personal uselessness...when called upon for help." This discouraging opinion was expressed recently by a chaplain, a psychologist and a psychiatrist who had worked together in the training of over 500 parish ministers.[1] Frequently the church leader is so unsure about what to do when people pour our their problems, these experts concluded, that he feels incompetent and highly insecure.

How does one build confidence and overcome these feelings of frustration and insecurity? One answer appears to be "time and experience." As he counsels with a variety of people and grows in maturity, the counselor becomes more proficient and self-assured. But this is not very comforting to the person who is just getting started, or to the one who has been counseling for several years and still feels a sense of frustration. The counselor may diligently apply all of the skills discussed in the preceding chapter and try to show good counselor characteristics, but at some time he will probably ask himself the question, "What do I do next?" This is the main concern of the present chapter: how we proceed from the beginning to the end in a counseling relationship. We begin with a consideration of the phases and types of counseling.

It is somewhat artificial to divide a counseling relationship into steps or phases because the boundaries between such phases are vague and there is considerable overlapping. Nevertheless, for the sake of discussion we can consider counseling as having contact, introductory, problem deliniation, solution, and termination phases. All these phases may take place in one interview or they may be spread over several meetings.

MAKING CONTACT

Obviously we can't counsel if we never come into contact with the people who need help. In launching a counseling ministry, therefore, we must begin by letting people know of our availability. This is commonly done in two ways: by announcing our willingness to counsel, and by informally demonstrating our concern.

Sometimes a formal announcement of one's availability can be printed in the church bulletin: "The pastor is available for counseling on Tuesdays and Thursdays. Please call the parsonage or church office for an appointment." At other times, casual comments can be made at meetings: "As advisers to this group, my wife and I are always happy to chat with anyone who wants to talk over a problem."

At the beginning such appeals are not likely to bring an avalanche of counselees. More often, formal counseling relationships grow out of informal contacts with people whom we meet at the church door or in the "marketplace."[2] For example, many young people are more likely to "open up" after they have come to know a youth leader on a basketball court or in some other informal setting. Chatting over coffee or on the way home from a meeting often gives prospective counselees an opportunity to casually raise a problem issue which might later be discussed in a more formal way. If continued discussion of the problem does seem wise, a comment like "Let's get together tomorrow

46

around 4 o'clock so we can discuss this further" is a casual but nevertheless effective way of making an appointment.

## THE INTRODUCTORY PHASE

At the beginning it is very important to put the counselee at ease and to establish *rapport*—"a comfortable...relationship of mutual confidence between two or more persons."[3] A pleasant setting and the presence of some of the counselor-counselee characteristics discussed in chapter 1 will help to get the relationship off to a good start. During the introductory phase there will be a mutual "sizing up" in which both counselor and counselee look each other over and make some tentative conclusions about their relationship. If the sizing up leads to some mutually positive feelings, the beginnings of rapport have been established.

Early in the interview the counselee is encouraged to describe some of his symptoms and tell why he has come for counseling. The counselor must spend most of his time listening and watching, which lets him get some picture of the person, his problems and his way of looking at the world, as well as permitting the counselee to release some of his bottled-up emotions.

## PROBLEM DELINIATION

As the counselee continues talking, we will begin to get some appreciation for his problems and, hopefully, come to see things from his point of view. The counselor might try to discover (by asking, if necessary) why the counselee has come for help, why he has come now, why he has come to him, what he expects from counseling, and what he has done to solve his problems in the past. In addition, the Christian counselor may want to know something about the counselee's spiritual background. Is he a believer? Has he invited Christ to be Lord of his life? Is he rebelling against his Christian upbringing?* As he talks, the counselee's statement of the

---

*Such questions, of course, are not asked in rapid-fire succession. They remain in the counselor's mind until the answers appear spontaneously or until there is opportunity to inquire, using the principles of wise questioning considered in chap. 1.

problem should be accepted tentatively, but we should also be alert to the possibility that the presented problem may not be the real problem.

This phase may take several counseling sessions, or it may only take a few minutes. Sometimes the counselor may feel that he doesn't fully understand why a problem has developed, but if he has a clear picture of what the problem is he is still capable of helping the counselee work toward its solution.

WORKING TOWARD SOLUTIONS

Beginning counselors often become very concerned lest they not be able to "find a solution" to the counselee's problem. This is a holdover from the idea that counseling is like a medical relationship in which the patient lists the symptoms and the doctor provides the cure.

But counseling is not usually like this. Instead, the counselee elaborates on his problem, and *both* the counselor and counselee try to work toward a solution. Often because of his objectivity, training and experience, the counselor will think of things that the counselee has never considered and many of these ideas will be discussed together by the participants. As both get greater insight into the situation, they might consider how the problem has been handled unsuccessfully in the past, and how it might be dealt with more effectively in the future. For example, the counselee sometimes may decide to make some practical change in his own behavior. At times he may recognize that it will be necessary to learn to live with a situation that cannot be altered. In pastoral counseling there will be a concern about the counselee's spiritual situation, and a consideration of how Christ can make a difference in troubled lives.

However, we must do more than talk about possible solutions. Each must be tried out and later evaluated by the counselee—with or without the counselor's help. If something doesn't work, we must look at the problem again and reevaluate our past thinking.

## TERMINATION

When both participants have an understanding of the problem, have "talked it out," and hopefully have arrived at some workable solutions, there is a mutual decision to end the counseling relationship. If the association has been long and pleasant, this may be difficult, especially for the counselee. Usually a comment like "I think we've almost reached the stage where you can work more on these problems by yourself" gives a hint to the counselee that the end is near. Then the participants can discuss together how the counselee can handle his problem with a minimum of outside help. This is the real goal of the whole counseling relationship: to assist the counselee to deal more effectively on his own with the problems of life.

On paper, all of this sounds concise and relatively easy, but it is much more difficult to apply in practice. It is helpful to remember that the counselor is not solely responsible for solving the problem but that counseling is a relationship in which at least two people are working *together* on an issue. It should also be remembered that the phases of counseling do not always proceed in order. Rapport is important during the entire counseling relationship, for example, and not just at the beginning. Frequently there is vascillation back and forth between the problem deliniation and solution stages. Then, it must be recognized that all problems are not handled in the same way. The lady who has just lost her husband needs a different kind of counseling than the teenager who is frustrated because the church youth program is irrelevant. The church leader, therefore, must have some appreciation for the different types of counseling.

## TYPES OF COUNSELING

Table 2-1 summarizes common types of counseling. With the exception of depth counseling, which should be used only by competent professionally trained counselors, all

## Table 2-1
## Types of Counseling*

### SUPPORTIVE

#### GOALS

1. To undergird, hold up, and stabilize troubled people.
2. To help the person gain strength and stability so he can cope with his problems.

#### SAMPLE PROBLEMS

1. Serious illness in the counselee or his family.
2. Death of a loved one.
3. Breakup of a marriage or engagement.
4. Failure of any kind.
5. Rejection by a significant person.
6. Severe disappointment.
7. Any other crisis.
8. Personal characteristics such as immaturity, inadequacy, or strong dependency.
9. Low intelligence or lack of desired abilities.

#### CHARACTERISTIC TECHNIQUES

1. Be a "shoulder to lean on." This involves reassuring, comforting, guiding and sustaining.
2. Be a "shoulder to cry on," listening while the counselee pours out his troubles.
3. Encourage the counselee to face his problem.
4. Give an objective view of the situation.
5. Help build up and support psychological defenses such as self-confidence.
6. Change the counselee's environment. This may, for example, involve removing him from a stressful home situation.
7. Encourage activity.
8. Utilize spiritual resources such as prayer, Scripture, devotional readings, etc.
9. Discuss the meaning of the counselee's problems.

#### POSSIBLE DANGERS

1. Overdependency by the counselee (especially if the second goal is ignored).
2. Encouraging the counselee to "wallow" in his problems.

### CONFRONTATIONAL

#### GOALS

1. Forcing the person to face and deal with some sin or difficult situation.
2. Helping him to develop the moral strength to avoid similar problems in the future.

#### SAMPLE PROBLEMS

1. Any illegal or immoral action, e.g., illegal drug use and possession, illegitimate pregnancy.
2. Any action which the individual, society, or Scripture considers to be wrong.

50

3. Any action which causes guilt feelings.
4. Dissenting factions in the church.

## CHARACTERISTIC TECHNIQUES

1. Confront the counselee with the evidence.
2. Support and accept him as a person.
3. Encourage confession to God and to the people he has wronged (Pr. 28:13; 1 Jn. 1:9; Ja. 5:16a.)
4. Give assurance of God's forgiveness (1 Jn. 1:9).
5. Help the counselee forgive himself.
6. Guide the counselee as he makes restitution (when this is possible).
7. Encourage alternate and more responsible ways of behaving.
8. Work to strengthen the conscience and self-control.
9. Guide spiritual growth.
10. Utilize prayer, Scripture reading, reliance on the Holy Spirit, etc.

## POSSIBLE DANGERS

1. Pride, or "one-up-manship" in the counselor.
2. Rejection of the counselee because of his actions.
3. Moralizing (lecturing about the counselee's behavior and ignoring most of the techniques in the previous column).
4. Not helping the counselee to change his behavior and to strengthen his controls.

## EDUCATIVE

### GOALS

1. Discovering, with the counselee, what information is needed.
2. Providing information or helping the counselee to find information.
3. Showing him how to find information on his own in the future.

### SAMPLE PROBLEMS

1. Vocational counseling.
2. Premarital guidance.
3. Marriage and family counseling.
4. Questions about theology or the Bible.
5. Social incompetence.
6. Requests for advice.
7. Troublesome behavior which the counselee does not understand
8. Tensions, problems and doctrinal divisions in the church.

### CHARACTERISTIC TECHNIQUES

1. Encourage questioning.
2. Be supportive if the question might be embarrassing to the counselee (e.g., teenagers asking sex questions).
3. Communicate information or direct the counselee to a source of information, such as a book or knowledgeable person.
4. Provide opportunity for discussion of the information.
5. Encourage the counselee to use the information when possible (e.g., information about dating should be used in dating situations).
6. Give encouragement and praise when genuine learning appears or when desirable changes in behavior occur.

characteristic techiques (continued)

7. Make suggestions which would help the counselee to gain insight into his behavior.
8. Be alert to other issues (since requests for information often hide more basic problems).

## POSSIBLE DANGERS

1. Counselee becoming overdependent on the counselor as a teacher.
2. Counselor belief that passing out information will always bring genuine learning or behavior change.
3. Counselor manipulation of the counselee (pressuring him to accept your ideas).
4. Domination of the counselee. This is easy if you are giving information, making interpretations, or teaching new ways of behaving.
5. Counselor thinking that he is an "expert" in some area, just because people ask for his advice.

# PREVENTATIVE

## GOALS

1. To anticipate problems before they arise.
2. To prevent worsening of existing problems.

## SAMPLE PROBLEMS

1. Youth with increasing sex drives.
2. High school students facing college.
3. Young people facing marriage, the military, etc.
4. People who are preparing to retire.
5. People facing surgery, serious illness, other crises, etc.

## CHARACTERISTIC TECHNIQUES

1. Be alert to the potential problems and dangers.
2. Confronting people with the dangers.
3. Educate in sermons, discussions, private talks, etc.
4. Avoid an all-knowing, "holier than thou," superior, or nontrusting attitude.
5. Be tactful.
6. Encourage discussion of potential problems.
7. Know suggested solutions or ways to avoid problems.
8. Be alert to relevant Scripture.

## POSSIBLE DANGERS

1. Ignoring the potential problem until it becomes serious.
2. Overdramatizing potential problems, making them sound worse than they really are.

# SPIRITUAL

## GOALS

1. To clarify the issues and find solutions to theological problems.
2. To help the counselee to find meaning and purpose to life.

3. To teach people how to grow spiritually.

## SAMPLE PROBLEMS

1. Problems of doubt, unbelief, and confusion.
2. Problems of emptiness, meaninglessness, or lack of purpose in life.
3. A desire to know God.
4. Confusion over the meaning of life crises.
5. Confusion and disagreement in the church over doctrinal issues.

## CHARACTERISTIC TECHNIQUES

1. Encourage free expression of problems, concerns and doubts.
2. Be honest in your reactions, beliefs, etc.
3. Avoid clichés and superficiality.
4. Be willing to discuss, to raise pertinent issues, and to confront.
5. Be alert to relevant Scripture and other sources of information.

6. Teach facts concerning spiritual rebirth and growth to spiritual maturity.
7. Point out spiritual needs in the counselee's life.
8. Utilize prayer, reliance on the Holy Spirit's guidance, etc.

## POSSIBLE DANGERS

1. Failure to recognize that theological questions may hide deeper problems.
2. Squelching with a cliché comment like "trust in the Lord and your problems will all disappear." (Paul trusted, but he still had a thorn in the flesh).
3. Tendency to read a few Bible verses and not deal with the real concerns of the counselee.
4. Assumption that spiritual problems are all the result of sin. For example, a desire to learn spiritual truths is not the result of sin (see Ac. 17:11).

## REFERRAL

### GOALS

1. To provide short-term support or other temporary help.
2. To refer the counselee to another counselor.

### SAMPLE PROBLEMS

1. The seriously disturbed.
2. The severely depressed or suicidal.
3. People who need long-term counseling.
4. Those whom you aren't helping.
5. People who need medical care.
6. People you strongly dislike.

7. People who need help in managing finances and budgeting.

### CHARACTERISTIC TECHNIQUES

1. Be alert to local referral sources (other pastors, professional counselors, community clinics, school counselors, etc).
2. Get to know some of these people.
3. Be able to provide information about referral sources and how to contact them.
4. Know who to refer (see the SPIRITUAL column).
5. Create the expectation for referral (e.g., "We may find that someone

characteristic techniques (continued)

else could handle this better."). Mention this early in any interview where referral seems possible.
6. Help the counselee to see the value of referral.
7. Be accepting (since referral is sometimes seen as rejection).

## POSSIBLE DANGERS

1. Counselee who thinks referral is really rejection.
2. Referring too quickly. Often the pastoral counselor can be of more help than he realizes.
3. Not referring when you have neither the competence, training, nor time to handle the problem.

# DEPTH

## GOALS

1. To uncover and deal with deep emotional problems.
2. To create counselee self-awareness and insight.
3. To restructure the personality.
4. To create more effective functioning.

## SAMPLE PROBLEMS

1. The severely disturbed.
2. People with deep personal problems, insecurities, depressions, social inadequacies, etc.

## CHARACTERISTIC TECHNIQUES

Techniques are varied and often highly technical. Depth counseling should be avoided by pastors unless they have specialized training in this area, and plenty of time for counseling.

## POSSIBLE DANGERS

1. Poorly trained people attempting depth counseling.

---

*Adapted from G. R. Collins, "The Pastor and His Counseling Service," in W. Kerr, *The Minister's Research Service* (Wheaton, Ill.: Tyndale, 1970), pp. 136-41; and H. J. Clinebell, *Basic Types of Pastoral Counseling* (Nashville, Tenn.: Abingdon, 1965.

of these could be used at times by church leaders. With any given counselee, one of these approaches may be used, or there could be a combination of several. For the young person who wants to know "what a minister's life is really like," educative counseling would be most appropriate. For the person who has a serious drinking problem, a combination of confrontational, educative, preventive, spiritual, and referral counseling might be helpful.

## SUPPORTIVE COUNSELING

The church leader, especially the pastor, often finds himself giving support and encouragement in times of need. There was a time when "tightly knit communities once furnished friends and neighbors who could stand by in moments of shock,...[but] in a society on wheels the task of providing such sustenance to urban and suburban people falls heavily upon the clergy" and members of the church.[4]

Supportive counseling is most often used with people who are having difficulty standing alone amid the problems of life. Some are "psychological cripples" who at frequent intervals need to be sustained with guidance and reassurance. Alcoholics, for example, often need such support, and they can get it in Alcoholics Anonymous. Others, who normally get along quite well, "fall apart" in times of crisis and need someone to lean on while they adjust to a disappointing failure, the loss of a loved one, or some other catastrophe.

In supportive counseling, the goal is not to encourage immature dependency on another person. Rather, the counselor gives temporary support and helps the person to "gain strength and perspective which will allow him to use his personality resources more effectively in coping with life situations."[5] To achieve this, discourage such unhealthy responses as denying that the problem exists; evading the problem through fantasy, alcohol, drugs, or other devices; refusing to seek or accept help; denying the existence of "negative" feelings such as hatred, anger anxiety, or guilt; refusing to consider realistic alternatives to the present situation; blaming others for one's problems; relying on others to cure the situation; and turning away from family and friends. It is more healthy if the counselee can be helped to face the problem realistically and attempt to understand it; express and discuss his resentments, guilt or other negative feelings; accept some responsibility for coping with the problem; explore various ways to handle the situation; recognize and accept the fact that some things cannot be changed (such as the departure of a loved one); communicate with relatives, friends and others; and take practical steps, however small, to handle the problem constructively.[6]

After working for several years with dying patients, one psychiatrist concluded that people like to avoid stressful and unpleasant situations by pretending that they don't exist.[7] We clench our teeth and persistently press on, sometimes believing that God will remove all of the problems if we wait long enough. But it is wiser and healthier to face the problems, commit them to God (Mt. 11:28-30), and then take practical steps toward their solution. The counselor can provide the support and encouragement that are needed if this growth is to take place.

## CONFRONTATIONAL COUNSELING

In His dealings with people, Jesus often confronted them with their sins. He confronted the rich young ruler with his overconcern for riches (Lk. 18:22), the Samaritan woman with her immorality (Jn. 4:17-18), His disciples with their little faith (Mt. 8:26; 14:31), and the religious leaders with their sin (Mt. 12:34; 15:7-8; 23:23-33; Jn. 8:44-45).

It is one thing for Jesus "who knew no sin" to be pointing out the sins of others, but it is quite another thing for Christians who have beams in their eyes to be confronting other men with their weaknesses. Some professional counselors feel nothing should be done to make counselees feel guilty or inadequate, but this view has been challenged by those who feel that the counselor should, at times, be willing to confess his own weaknesses, and to confront the counselee with his misdeeds.[8]

The debate may go on in professional circles, but for the Christian it is clear that we must encourage people to face up to their sins. Hiding one's immoral actions only creates guilty frustration and neurotic anxiety. If we confess our sins, God will forgive (1 Jn. 1:9) and we will obtain mercy (Pr. 28:13). As a servant of God, the counselor must help the counselee to face his sins, to confess them, and to do something about changing himself.

## EDUCATIVE COUNSELING

Most human behavior is learned behavior. We learn how to talk, think, dress, and act in social situations. When problems come into our lives we draw upon past learning to work out a solution, or we avoid the problems by using defensive mechanisms or other learned escapist techniques. Mental patients show symptoms which are, for the most part, learned ways of coping with stress. Any behavior—however unusual—that has been successful in reducing anxiety in the past will continue to be used in the future.

If so much behavior has been learned, it seems reasonable to assume that counseling should consist primarily of education in which the ineffective behavior is unlearned and the counselee learns new more appropriate ways of acting.[9] This approach to counseling, a significant development in the field, holds that the counselor is really a teacher, not a doctor, and that the counselee is a student rather than a patient.

Whether or not *all* counseling is basically relearning is another issue for debate, but there can be no doubt that *much* of the pastoral counselor's work involves education. People with theological questions, concerns about marriage and vocational choice, or requests for advice, are really seeking information. Young people who are social misfits must learn how to act appropriately in social situations.

People who are faced with an important decision may seek the church leader's opinion and guidance.

It is flattering to realize that someone thinks of us as an expert on some topic and values our advice. When thrust into this role, therefore, many people show a tendency to give opinions, even on subjects about which they know nothing. In educative counseling we must maintain a spirit of humility and make it our practice to look to the authoritative Word of God whenever this has a bearing on the problem. We should ask God for wisdom as we help others with their problems and we must, at times, confess that we don't know the answer but will seek to find it as we work on the problem along with the counselee. The principles of human learning, which will be discussed in a later volume in this series, apply to counseling as much as they apply to the more formal programs of Christian education.

## PREVENTIVE COUNSELING

Counseling does not exist solely for the purpose of getting people out of trouble. Sometimes its goal is to keep people from getting into trouble. Marriage counseling, for example, is usually concerned about helping partners who are having difficulty in getting along, but premarital counseling tries to anticipate problems before they arise and to help couples avoid or deal with potentially disruptive situations. The latter is preventive counseling. In it an attempt is made to anticipate problems before they arise or to deal with beginning problems before they get worse.

In our society people are not always enthusiastic about accepting unsolicited advice. This is especially true of youth who, as those most able to profit from the advice of others, are the least inclined to accept it. Making decisions on one's own is a commonly accepted mark of being "grown up," but a willingness to consider the advice of more experienced people is a less widely accepted but even greater mark of maturity. With these considerations in mind, the counselor who wants to prevent problems from developing must often use extreme tact. He must avoid an attitude of superiority and must not convey the paternalistic idea that "if you don't do this, you'll be sorry." Often an issue can be raised and then discussed in a rational manner. "Have you had a chance yet to discuss how you will handle finances?" is a better approach in premarital counseling than a statement like "Let me give you some points about handling money."

### SPIRITUAL COUNSELING

In one sense all pastoral counseling is really spiritual counseling. As followers of Christ, we are duty bound to make disciples of all men and to help those who are weak (Mt. 28:19-20; Ro. 15:1; Gal. 6:1-2; 1 Th. 5:14). Because of this, we cannot be timid in raising spiritual issues, even when the presented problem seems to be of a nonspiritual nature (such as a request for information). A question like "How are things going spiritually?" can often introduce the spiritual issue when it has not come up otherwise. Sometimes the counselor has opportunity for introducing men to Jesus Christ or for encouraging people to commit their lives to the lordship of Christ. Often he will pray with the counselee or read a passage from the Bible. This kind of counseling can lead to a more satisfying life on earth (Jn. 10:10) and to eternal life in heaven (Jn. 3:16).

In helping people find meaning and purpose in life, the religious counselor has no peer. Even Freud recognized this. "Only religion," he wrote, "is able to answer the question of the purpose of life. One can hardly go wrong in concluding that the idea of a purpose in life stands and falls with the religious system."[10] In view of this it is regretful that many pastoral counselors avoid raising these ultimate issues in counseling and sometimes dodge them when they do arise.

It must be recognized, however, that what appears to be

a spiritual issue is often a cover for a deeper psychological problem. Hospitalized psychotics often talk about having committed the unpardonable sin, for example, but the nature of the problem is likely to be more psychological than spiritual. It is also true that many people develop psychological problems as a cover for their spiritual problems. "I can't concentrate on my studies" sounds like a psychological problem, but it *may* indicate an underlying spiritual struggle that is sapping one's energy. Of course, we shouldn't assume that all problems are spiritually caused—the causes of the problems are varied and complex—but the fact that the counselee has chosen a religious counselor may indicate that there is a conscious or unconscious spiritual need.

I am reminded of a long-distance telephone call which I received late one night from a man in San Francisco who wanted to fly to the Midwest to talk about a problem of persistent depression. After we had talked for a while, he remarked, "There are hundreds of psychologists in San Francisco, but I came to you because I knew you would at some time ask about my spiritual condition." He had not mentioned this initially and had even appeared uneasy when I brought up the subject. The pastoral counselor, therefore, "must be tuned simultaneously to the horizontal and vertical dimensions of *every human problem*."[11]

REFERRAL COUNSELING

It is not an admission of failure or incompetence to refer a counselee to someone better trained to handle a problem. Counseling often requires time and specialized counselor skills which the busy church leader may lack, but he can perform a valuable service in helping troubled people find the specialized professional help they need.

On arrival in a new community, a pastor should begin a file of competent specialists to whom counselees could be referred by himself and by laymen involved in counseling.

Psychologists and psychiatrists will be included in the list of specialists, but these are not the only people to whom counselees are referred. Medical doctors, gynecologists, vocational counselors, social workers, lawyers and others should be included in the referral file, as should the names of key people in local mental health clinics and other community agencies. Often other pastors or established residents of the community and church can give suggestions for the file.

There are several basic guidelines for making referrals. First, the counselor must keep the counselee's best welfare in mind. If we ask at every stage, "What is best for him?" the referral is likely to be smoother. Second, the referral must be done in such a way that the counselee does not feel rejected. Frequently it takes considerable courage for a counselee to come and talk about a personal problem. The fact that he came to you indicates that, in his opinion, you are the person who can help best; so when you suggest referral, he may feel rejection and discouragement because the counselor he most trusts cannot help. To make referral easier, the counselor must do everything he can to reassure the counselee that this is the best way to deal with the problem. If referral seems like even a remote possibility, you should mention early in the interview that someone else might be of greater help. This creates an expectation for referral, and makes for a smoother transition later. Third, the counselee should be part of the decision to refer. The counselor can discuss the situation with him, outline what other help is available, and indicate why it might be better to refer. Most counselors believe that the counselee should take the initiative in making an appointment with the new counselor although a telephone conversation between counselors (with the counselee's permission) can often help to pave the way for referral and to insure that the referral source is available to help at this time. Finally, the church leader should maintain a concern about the counselee and his welfare. Someone else may be doing the counseling, but the church leader is still interested.[12]

## DEPTH COUNSELING

Depth counseling is a long-term relationship in which a counselee's deep-seated problems are uncovered and considered in detail. There is no reason why this could not be a part of the church leader's work "if he were trained, had the time, and did not in the process step out of his role as a pastor. That is, extended counseling is not inherently foreign to the pastorship, but in a practical sense it is rarely wise or appropriate for most pastors (or other church leaders) to engage in it."[13] This is because depth counseling is a highly skilled and time-consuming process. Some church leaders have these skills, but such people are almost always professional counselors in addition. The minister or non-psychologist layman, therefore, has another calling and should avoid playing with depth counseling.

## INFORMAL COUNSELING

Counseling doesn't always take place in the formal atmosphere of a pastor's study. On the contrary, a great deal—perhaps most—of pastoral counseling is informal. It takes place over coffee, in a hospital room, during informal home visits, or in the hallway after a meeting. Opportunities for informal counseling are legion, especially if the church leader is sensitive to subtle signs of distress (such as a decline in church attendance, depression, an avoidance of people, frequent intoxication, or any other unusual or different behavior), and if he uses casual statements to get the person talking (e.g., "How are things going?" "You look tired today," "How have you been getting along spiritually?" "How do you feel today?" "I've wondered if something's been bothering you lately."). When people sense your concern and willingness to listen, they will often "open up."

In one of his books on pastoral counseling, Clinebell

suggests nine things to do during informal contacts:

1. Listen intensively.
2. Use questions carefully to focus on conflict areas rapidly.
3. Help the person review the total problem. This tends to produce a clearer perspective and prepare the person to make an enlightened decision. It also helps him to mobilize his inner resources.
4. Provide useful information.
5. Focus on the major conflict, problem, or area of decision with the aim of clarifying viable alternatives.
6. Help the person decide on the "next step" and then take it.
7. Provide guidance when it seems useful.
8. Give the person emotional support and inspiration.
9. Move into longer-term counseling if brief counseling does not prove adequate.[14]

This informal counseling may not seem to be very important, but it has helped innumerable people. It is a way of ministering to the needy and, in so doing, we are serving the risen Christ (Mt. 25:37-40).

## GROUP COUNSELING

Groups have provided an effective vehicle for pastoral counseling. By meeting with several counselees at once, the group leader makes better use of his time and, more important, provides an environment where a number of people can work together to honestly show their feelings and help each other with problems.

This was very dramatically illustrated in a marriage counseling group which I once led. All of the couples in the group were having marital difficulties, and at one session there was a verbal explosion between one of the men and his wife. They called each other names, shook fists, and did everything short of beating each other over the head. The other group members watched uncomfortably and then discussed what had happened. The feuding couple had the insights and reactions of the observers who, in turn, learned what "we must look like when we fight." This experience was very helpful to everyone and was a topic of much discussion during the sessions which followed.

Group counseling has greatly increased during the past several years. Alcoholics Anonymous, which began in the late '30s, now has group meetings all over the world. After World War II, group therapy became popular as a treatment technique, and "T-groups" got started as a procedure in which people could probe the strengths and weaknesses of each other's personalities. In the '60s, family counseling groups began springing up, and now in the '70s, marathon groups—which last for several hours—and nude therapy groups (for which no description is needed) are enjoying great popularity.

Christian group meetings began with the twelve disciples and were a typical characteristic of the early believers. In these church groups, which existed for the purpose of study, fellowship, communion services and prayer, the participants shared their possessions with each other, worshiped together, ate together, and spent time praising God (Ac. 2:42-47). Today there is a small-group explosion in the church as more and more believers are meeting together to share their experiences, to confess their faults, to pray (Ja. 5:16) and to study the Scriptures together.[15]

Group counseling in the church has been hailed as an exciting advance for pastoral counseling. This is especially true when the group is led by someone who is competent and well trained in group-counseling methods. But there is also danger in this! In an attempt to be honest and authentic, it is easy to be vicious and inconsiderate. Some "honesty groups" are

harmful and almost invariably wind up being *un*Christian.

The object of honesty...is not to reveal immoral and lascivious incidents. The object is rather to begin to acknowledge to God and to each other the true nature of the personal struggles of living in the world today, so that we can begin to find freedom, healing, and forgiveness—and provide a place where others can experience these things. One does not rip off his mask (or anyone else's). Rather he becomes willing for God to remove the unnecessary part of his facade gradually by providing the security he needs to be more honest. Also a ground rule in this type of group is never to share something in such a way that it may make *another* person vulnerable. The highest value in the Christian life is not honesty—but *love* (I Corinthians 13).[16]

How does one get group counseling started in the church? Suggestions are given in chapter 6 for starting small study-discussion groups, and many of the same principles apply for groups of people with problems.

Before suggesting group counseling, a personal interview should be held with each participant. This allows the group counselor to get some understanding of the problem and permits him to evaluate how the counselee might fit into a group. If group counseling seems advisable, a few minutes should be spent discussing this with the counselee and giving him some idea of what to expect from a group.

When the group meets for the first time, the counselor may suggest some broad guidelines, such as honest sharing in love, or that group discussion be kept confidential and not reported with nongroup members. The twelve practical guidelines discussed in chapter 6 should be kept in mind and several might be mentioned. Then some time should be spent in introductions, followed perhaps by a discussion of the anxiety that most people feel at the beginning of a group experience. Slowly people will begin to share their experiences and later their feelings and problems. At times they also may wish to pray together for God's guidance.

The counselor who serves as a group leader is both a participant, an observer and a catalyst. At times he expresses his own feelings, but he also tries to stimulate discussion, to occasionally summarize what is going on, and to keep the participants from wandering too far from the topic. He also may intentionally limit the depth of interaction by discouraging the expression of highly personal feelings.[17] The sharing of such feelings might be acceptable in depth-therapy groups, but it is best avoided in church counseling.

Some groups agree to terminate their relationship after a specified number of meetings. Other groups continue indefinitely but membership changes as new people join and older participants "drop out"—hopefully because counseling is no longer needed. At periodic intervals the counselor and sometimes the group as a whole should pause to evaluate how things are going and how the group experience could be more helpful to the participants.

## The Church's Counseling Program

Although many people bring their problems to the church, it should always be remembered that the church is not primarily a mental health agency. Every Christian leader must ask, therefore, how the church can minister to the counseling needs of people but still carry on with its other programs of witness and work. Here are four steps in this direction:

*Train pastors in counseling.* The American Association of Pastoral Counselors has listed the desired requirements for a competent pastoral counselor. These include college and seminary degrees, a master's degree in pastoral counseling, ordination, and good standing in one's denomination, three years of parish experience, six months of clinical training, 150 hours of supervised counseling, and personal therapy.

The average pastor or missionary is likely to throw up his

hands in despair after reading this list, but many men are effective counselors even though they have not achieved these high standards. Most seminaries and other training institutions now offer required courses in counseling and there are frequently "pastor's courses" for men who are active in the ministry but in need of more counselor training. The professional church leader should take advantage of these educational opportunities and read broadly in the area of pastoral psychology and counseling.

*Train laymen in counseling.* The layman is often in a very crucial position for doing counseling, especially of the informal type. The pastor or professional Christian counselor can often train some of these men and women in theology, in basic psychology, and in effective counseling techniques. Such training is best restricted to more mature Christian leaders who naturally show some of the characteristics of good counselors. The person who cannot keep confidences, or the one who appears to have personal hangups that he would be working out in counseling relationships, should be discouraged from counseling and encouraged to serve in some other part of the church's program.

*Work to establish Christian counseling centers.* Some large churches are able to employ a minister of counseling whose training and skills enable him to function effectively as a counseling specialist. Where such a ministry is not feasible, several churches might pool their resources to hire such a man, or several men who could form the nucleus of a Christian counseling center.

The counselors in such settings could be responsible for individual and group counseling, vocational and marital counseling, and the training of lay counselors. The specialist could also advise Christian education committees as they plan their church programs and participate in training programs and church meetings.

While this is ideal, it is also an almost unattainable goal. Few men and women are both competent counselors and committed Christians. This situation will change as seminaries and graduate schools train more counselors, but for a long time to come only a few churches will have the luxury of a minister of counseling or a nearby Christian counseling center.

*Evaluate frequently.* As faithful Christian stewards, we must pause frequently to evaluate what we are doing—both as individual counselors and as a local church. To do this adequately would require the use of sophisticated research techniques, but casual evaluation can also be helpful.

After each interview, ask yourself, What did I do that was good? What did I do that was poor? How could I have improved the counseling? If the counselee has given permission for a tape recording to be made of the session, you can listen to this with a critical ear.

At a more general level, church leaders can periodically ask themselves if they are meeting the needs of the people, helping them with their problems, and assisting them in their spiritual growth. Sometimes a carefully designed questionnaire can give invaluable feedback which helps as future programs are planned.

As humans we will never really be able to evaluate the effectiveness of our counseling ministry as long as we are present here on earth. But we have a responsibility to be as capable as we can while there is still time to work.

## SUMMARY

After someone pours out his problems in a counseling interview, what do we do next—besides panic? The answer will depend somewhat on the counselee and on the problem. After we have made a start at building a comfortable relationship, we should try, with the counselee, to delineate the problem. First, consider what solutions have been tried in the past, if any, and then talk about what might be tried in the future. Sometimes we will give a lot of support and

68

encouragement. At other times we might confront the counselee with some sin or self-defeating behavior, help him to learn more effective ways of behaving in the future, guide him away from potential problems, or discuss his spiritual condition. In some situations we will recognize that we lack the time, skill and/or knowledge to help the person and we will assist him to get counseling elsewhere. After we have discussed the issue, we will assist the counselee to face his problems without the aid of a counselor. This whole process may be very brief and informal—lasting for ten minutes over a cup of coffee—or it may go on for several months, or even years. Recently there has been an upsurge of interest in group counseling wherein a counselor meets with several counselees.

Although this is not their prime responsibility or concern, counseling will continue to be a big responsibility for church leaders. The counseling will be more effective if pastors and laymen are trained in counseling techniques, if church programs can be designed to help stimulate mental health, if professional Christian counseling can be made available, and if the counseling program can be reevaluated at frequent intervals.

## 3
# Premarital, Marital, and Family Counseling

When God created the heavens and the earth, He concluded that human beings should be of two sexes, male and female (Gen. 1:27). Adam and Eve became the first married couple and soon they began raising children. Beginning with their example, the importance of marriage and the family is stressed time and time again throughout the pages of Scripture. The family is mentioned in all sixty-six books of the Bible; guidelines for successful family living appear frequently (see especially Eph. 5:22—6:4); and there are numerous examples of family relationships. The Bible describes the family backgrounds of great leaders such as Abraham, Isaac, Jacob, Joseph, Moses, Samuel, David, John the Baptist, and a host of others, including Jesus Himself. Although He never married, Jesus clearly approved of marriage. It was at a wedding that He performed His first miracle (Jn. 2:1-11) and later He commented on the ideal of Christian marriage as a lifelong union in which two people become one (Mk. 10:5-9).

Few people reach this ideal today. Almost one-third of all marriages in our society end in divorce, and of the marriages which do persist, an unknown number are characterized by frustration and unhappiness. In a survey conducted several years ago it was found that 50 percent of all people who came to a pastor for counseling did so because of marriage or family problems.[1] More recently in their surveys of church youth, Strommen and Zuck and Getz found that young people listed dating and marriage as the topics for which, more than any other, they wanted help from the church.[2] It is hardly surprising, then, that Clinebell, after reviewing the whole issue of marriage and family counseling, concluded that proficiency in this area should be the church leader's "most indispensable counseling skill."[3]

## Premarital Counseling

The time to begin work on marriage and family problems is before they ever arise. Ideally, preparation for marriage begins when one is a small child. If the parents have a good marriage, the children learn attitudes and ways of behaving which enable them in turn to also have happy marriages.[4]

Regardless of one's home background, however, the decision to marry is of major importance and many couples approach their wedding day with feelings of both expectant enthusiasm and fearful hesitation. By helping people at this critical time in their lives, the church leader is often able to make a significant contribution to the future success of these marriages.

### GOALS OF PREMARITAL COUNSELING

Premarital counseling seeks to help individuals, couples, and groups of couples to prepare for and build happy and successful marriages. Just as preventive medicine attempts to prevent disease and point people toward health, so premarital guidance seeks to anticipate difficulties in marriage and family living and to help people build healthy, satisfying marriage relationships.[5] In counseling with people prior to marriage, at least five goals are of special importance:[6]

*Assessing readiness for marriage*. While there is no concise formula by which to determine if a person is ready for marriage, here are some broad indicators which the counselor should bear in mind:

1.  The reasons for marriage. An engaged couple may present any number of sound reasons for getting married, including love, an awareness of God's leading, or a desire for companionship and sexual fulfillment. Sometimes, however, the stated reasons are such that a marriage would be unwise. It is especially difficult for a husband and wife to build a good relationship if they marry primarily as a response to social pressure, to show revenge against a parent or former partner, to avoid the stigma of being an "old maid," to get away from an unhappy home, to satisfy sexual infatuation, or because the girl is pregnant.

2.  The degree of background similarity. A marriage is more likely to be successful when a couple have similar interests and values, come from the same socioeconomic class and similar family backgrounds, are of the same race, have a similar amount of education, and are of the same religious faith.[7]

3.  Age. A number of research studies have shown that teenage marriages are not very stable and end in divorce much more often than do marriages between couples who are older.[8] The reasons for this are complex but it appears that early marriages frequently involve people who are pregnant (it has been estimated that between one-third to one-half of all teenage brides are pregnant), from lower socioeconomic classes, or poorly educated. These marriages are plagued with problems from the beginning and the participants are often not mature enough to handle the stress. Maturity does not always come automatically with age, but the older one gets, the greater is the likelihood that one can establish and maintain personal relationships and effectively meet the problems of life.[9]

4.  In addition to age in terms of years, there is also the issue of age differences. In our society the husband is usually two or three years older than the wife, but an age difference of a few years either way rarely causes marital problems. Difficulties are more likely if the couple is ten

or more years apart. In such cases there are often dissimilarities in interests and physical vigor, a difficulty in finding mutual friends, and a tendency for the older person to act as parent rather than a spouse.[10]

5. Courtship. The period of courtship and engagement is an important predictor of later marital success. The couple who have known each other for a short time, or those whose courtship has been stormy and characterized by frequent conflict, are not ready for marriage.[11]

6. Attitudes toward marriage. If a person is afraid of or repulsed by thoughts of sexual intercourse, if there is a strong fear of marriage, if there is disagreement about whether or not to have children, if the prospective bride and groom have different views of the roles that each will assume in marriage, or if there are differing plans and expectations for the future, then it would surely be wise to postpone the wedding until these attitudes can be "talked through," perhaps with a counselor's help.

7. External circumstances. Sometimes there are circumstances in life which put added strain on a young marriage. These include demands of further schooling, existence of large debts, pressures of limited finances, parental opposition, or the prospect of military service with its necessity for separation and travel.[12] Some people, such as graduate students, may weigh the issues and decide to get married in spite of the difficulties; others prefer to wait. In either case these circumstantial issues must be considered in any determination of readiness to marry.

8. Spiritual maturity. Regardless of the above considerations, an individual is not ready for *Christian* marriage if he is an unbeliever, if he wants to marry a non-Christian, or if he is not completely yielded to the lordship of Jesus Christ. When we become believers we give ourselves to Christ, we become His children, and seek to do His will. If we marry someone who has a different commitment, either the marriage will suffer or our Christian service will

be less effective. It is important, therefore, that the believer seek another of like precious faith and that they walk together as one, serving Christ together. This mutual spiritual concern is no guarantee of automatic marital success (Christians and non-Christians alike can have problems and must work at marriage), but there are sure to be difficulties if one seeks to be a committed believer while "unequally yoked" with one who is spiritually dead (2 Co. 6:14).

*Anticipated potential stress.* Closely associated with determining a person's readiness for marriage is the task of identifying potential areas of stress. When two people of the opposite sex with different family backgrounds and varied past experiences begin to share life together, there are sure to be some adjustment problems. If these can be anticipated before marriage, the adjustment is likely to be much easier.

Issues which put stress on a marriage will differ from one couple to another, but some problems are especially common. In one widely reported study of several hundred married people, for example, it was found that sexual adjustment, the handling of finances, the choice of social and recreational activities, problems of getting along with the in-laws, differences in religious values or beliefs, and conflicts over the choice of friends—in that order—were the most difficult areas of marital adjustment. [13] Long before the wedding day, a prospective bride and groom should be alerted to these issues and encouraged to discuss them openly, honestly and at length. The attitudes and expectations that each has about these problem areas should be aired, with attempts made to resolve existing conflicts. It is not of great importance whether the issues are discussed by the couple alone, with other engaged persons in a group, or in the presence of a counselor. What *is* important is that the issues get discussed in depth, and that accurate factual knowledge be available for those who need it.

If the counselor is to help couples anticipate the stresses

of marriage, he would be wise to also encourage them to give careful thought to the honeymoon. Many years ago the necessity of a honeymoon was pointed out succinctly in a book by David Mace:

> From one point of view, getting married could be represented as a rather terrifying experience. For something like a third of their lifespan two people have lived independent of each other—probably without even knowing of each other's existence. They have formed their own personal habits and learned to live their own private lives. Now, after a comparatively short acquaintance, they come together in the closest human intimacy, living together, sleeping together, yielding themselves up to each other. At the time, they don't think of this as an invasion of their privacy. Their strong desire for each other draws them together and they make their surrender eagerly. But for all that, the mutual unveiling of their bodies and minds can sometimes have profoundly disturbing and quite unexpected consequences.... To make these early adjustments as easy as possible, we have wisely provided the institution of the honeymoon. [14]

The honeymoon is a transition stage between single and married life. It is an opportunity for the newly married couple to relax alone with each other and to start—psychologically and physically—to get used to their new status. However, even when a honeymoon is carefully planned and eagerly anticipated, there is always a degree of awkwardness. Inhibitions take time to overcome and it is probable that, in spite of the joys of the honeymoon, sexual adjustments during those first few days are at the poorest level that they will ever be. [15] Undressing in front of each other and engaging in the first act of sexual intercourse can be exciting, but it is also embarrassing and in many cases frustrating. In one study of Christian couples, only 31 percent reported that they were completely free of anxieties and fears on their wedding night.[16] It is important, therefore, that the details and mutual expectations for the honeymoon not be ignored in the discussions prior to marriage. If the church leader is uncomfortable about discussing these issues, he should refer the couple to someone who can discuss sex and the honeymoon without embarrassment. Of course, details of physiology can often be answered best by the physician who conducts the physical examinations which all couples should have prior to marriage.

It cannot be emphasized too strongly that most of the problems before and during marriage can be adequately met if a couple learns to communicate. Certainly it takes effort to listen carefully, to try to understand accurately, and to express oneself honestly in an attitude of love and mutual respect. The end result, however, is a smoother marital relationship, and this makes the effort worthwhile. Communication of one's attitudes, feelings, frustrations and uncertanties is as important as the communication of love and respect, but such communication does not start on the honeymoon. It begins long before marriage and the premarital counselor should do everything in his power to encourage and guide in the development of communication ability.

*Guiding self-evaluation.* In any interpersonal situation— including marriage—relationships are likely to be smoother if the participants are able to take an honest look at themselves. Jesus may have had this in mind when He told His followers to look at the beams in their own eyes before picking out the flaws in others (Mt. 7:3-5). The problem with this is that self-appraisal is painful and likely to make us feel uncomfortable. Nobody likes to face up to his own faults; it's much easier to criticize somebody else. When disagreements arise during the engagement period and later in marriage, the natural tendency is to self-righteously blame the other for most if not all of the problems, and then to push for one's own way. It never occurs to some people that at least partially they might be causing the problem themselves.

During the engagement period it is important for the couple—individually, with each other, and in the presence of a counselor—to work at seeing themselves more clearly. This means listing one's strong and weak characteristics, and trying to determine what attitudes, values, prejudices and aspirations are present. All of this takes considerable time, but it is worth the effort for the individual who wants to get his marriage off to a good start. Table 3-1 lists some of the issues that might be discussed as a couple seeks to evaluate themselves and their readiness to marry.

*Considering biblical views of marriage.* Shortly after man was created, God made woman. "It is not good that the man should be alone," the Creator decreed, so He instituted marriage and declared that a man should "cleave unto his wife: and they should be one flesh" (Gen. 2:18, 24).

Throughout the pages of the Bible there are a number of statements concerning the divine ideal for marriage. When a Christian couple are preparing to commit themselves to each other as husband and wife they have an obligation to know both what God expects of married couples and that He knows what is best for them as they unite with each other.

Table 3-2 summarizes the New Testament teachings concerning relationships within the family. With the help of the pastoral counselor, the couple should carefully discuss these divine ideals, especially as they are outlined in Ephesians 5:21—6:4, Colossians 3:16-21, 1 Corinthians 7, and 1 Peter 3:1-7. Since the relationship of the husband and wife is modeled after the bond that Christ has with His church, the latter should also be fully understood. Such an understanding makes it easier for many Christians to accept and appreciate such passages as those which instruct the wife to be in submission to her husband. In these days of Women's Liberation, the biblical view is very unpopular

# Table 3-1

## Premarital Self-Evaluation Questionnaire*

The following questions are designed to help couples think about themselves and about their readiness for marriage. There are no right or wrong answers. Each person should answer by drawing a circle around the "yes," the "no," or the "?" Try to use the question mark only when there is real uncertainty. After the questionnaire has been carefully completed, the couple should discuss their answers with each other and with their counselor.

Yes No ? 1. Even though you may accept advice from your parents, do you make important decisions for yourself?

Yes No ? 2. Are you often homesick when you are away from home?

Yes No ? 3. Do you ever feel embarrassed or uneasy in giving or receiving affection?

Yes No ? 4. Are your feelings easily hurt by criticism?

Yes No ? 5. Do you enjoy playing or working with small children?

Yes No ? 6. Do you feel embarrassed or uneasy in conversations about sex with older persons or members of the other sex?

Yes No ? 7. Do you have a clear understanding of the physiology of sexual intercourse and reproduction?

Yes No ? 8. Do you understand the psychological factors determining good sexual adjustment?

Yes No ? 9. Have you had the experience of using some of your earnings to help meet the expenses of others?

Yes No ? 10. In an argument, do you lose your temper easily?

Yes No ? 11. Have you and your fiancee ever worked through disagreements to a definite conclusion agreeable to both of you?

Yes No ? 12. Can you postpone something you want for the sake of later enjoyment?

**Yes** **No** ? 13. Are you normally free from jealousy?

Yes No ? 14. Have you thought carefully about the goals you will strive for in your marriage?

Yes No ? 15. Do you sometimes feel rebellious toward facing the responsibilities of marriage, occupational, or family life?

Yes No ? 16. Have you been able to give up gracefully something you wanted very much?

Yes No ? 17. Do you think of sexual intercourse as a pleasurable experience?

Yes No ? 18. Do you find it difficult to differ from others on matters of conduct or dress, even though you disagree with what they think?

Yes No ? 19. Do you often have to fight to get your way?

Yes No ? 20. Do you often find yourself making biting remarks, or using sarcasm toward others?

Yes No ? 21. Do you find yourself strongly emphasizing the glamour aspects of marriage, e.g., the announcement, congratulations, showers, the wedding?

Yes No ? 22 Have you and your fiance (fiancée) associated with each other in a variety of nonamusement situations, e.g., caring for children, in a work project, in time of stress?

Yes No ? 23. Have you and your fiance (fiancée) discussed matters which might cause marital conflict? For example: (underline those you have discussed) religious differences; plans for having children; attitudes toward sex; differences in family background; financial arrangements in marriage (such as your views on insurance, savings, budgeting, credit buying, giving to the church); attitudes toward living many miles from parents if necessary; occupational and educational plans; recreational preferences; attitudes toward each other's family; preferences for friends; basic values in life, etc.

Yes No ? 24. Have you been married or engaged before?

Yes No ? 25. Can you state why you want to get married?

Yes No ? 26. Have you prayed about your marriage and committed it to divine control?

*Adapted with permission from L. A. Kirkendall, *Marriage and Family Relations* (Dubuque, Ia.: Brown, 1965).

## Table 3-2

## New Testament Teachings on Relationships

## Within the Family*

A. Husband and Wife
    I. The marital relationship arranged by God
        1. The teachings of Jesus: Gen. 2:24 (quoted); Mk. 10:2-12 (cf. Mt. 19:3-12)
        2. The teachings of Paul: 1 Co. 7:2; 1 Ti. 6:3 (asceticism rebuked)
        3. Other teachings: Heb. 13:4
    II. Life within the marital relationship
        Heb. 13:4
        1 Co. 7:1-5 (There is to be no practice of abstinence within the marriage relationship except by mutual consent, for a brief season, and for devotional purposes. Even this is by consent, not command.)
        1 Co. 7:34-35 (Although Paul is advising against marriage under certain circumstances, he is nevertheless giving a true picture of the attitude of a good wife toward her husband.)
        Eph. 5:21-33 (Paul's purpose here is to speak of the church, but his high concept of the marital relation is evident.)
        Col. 3:18-19
        1 Ti. 5:8
        Titus 2:4-5 and perhaps 6
    III. Questions about divorce
        1. Basic teachings of Jesus: 1 Co. 7:10-11; Mk. 10:2-12; Mt. 19:3-12; Lk. 16:18
        2. Teachings of Jesus applied in unfavorable circumstances: Mt. 5:31-32 (Apparently "saving for the cause of fornication" is an interpretation of eventual circumstances.); 1 Co. 7:12-17 (Paul does not advise divorce in the case of a Christian married to a non-Christian except under most unfavorable circumstances. In such cases, the Christian has not been bound as he or she is bound according to 7:10-11.)
    IV. Questions on remarriage after divorce
        Mk. 6:17-19 (cf. Lev. 20-21)
        1 Co. 7:15
        1 Ti. 3:2, 12
        Titus 1:6
        1 Ti. 5:9
        Lk. 16:18
        Cf. also Mt. 5:32; 19:9

V. Questions on the advisability of marriage
   1. Marriage of Christians and non-Christians forbidden: 2 Co. 6:14; 1 Co.
      7:39
   2. Marriage under some circumstances inadvisable: 1 Co. 7:25-38 (The cir-
      cumstances are not defined; they are mentioned in 7:26. Paul's intention
      seems to be that the Christian should create no further obligations but
      devote himself to God instead.)
   3. Marriage of widowers (?) and widows permitted but not encouraged:
      1 Co. 7:8-9 (but cf. 1 Ti. 5:9-14, *per contra*); 1 Co. 7:39-40; Ro. 7:1-4 (This
      passage is illustrating another point.)
   4. Marriage of most people, including some widows and/or widowers, ad-
      visable: 1 Co. 7:1-2; 7-9; 1 Ti. 5:11-15
   VI. Other references to betrothal, marriage, and the marital relationship merely
       illustrative: Mk. 2:19-20; Jn. 2
B. Parent and Child
   I. Parents' responsibility
      2 Ti. 1:5
      Eph. 6:4; Col. 3:21
      Lk. 11:11-13; 2 Co. 6:18; Eph. 5:1 (The idea of God as Father gives instruc-
      tion as to what fatherhood should mean.)
      Lk. 2 (This chapter, like other material in both Old and New Testaments,
      teaches by example.)
   II. Child's responsibility
      Lk. 18:20; Eph. 6:2-3
      Eph. 6:1; Col. 3:20
      Mk. 7:10-12; Mt. 15:4-6
      Cf. 1 Ti. 5:1-2
C. Widows
   1 Ti. 5:16; Ja. 1:27; 1 Ti. 5:3-7, 9-10
D. Other
   1 Ti. 5:1-2 (The use of "brothers" as a name of Christians points up the significance of this relationship. Cf. the story of Mary, Martha, and Lazarus.)

---

*Adapted with permission from W. E. Oates, *Premarital Pastoral Care and Counseling*
(Nashville: Broadman, 1958), pp. 15-18.

and even Christians prefer to eliminate "obey" from the wedding ceremony. But the husband's being "head of the wife" does not imply aggressive and cruel domination. Instead, it means a sacrificial and giving love like that described in 1 Corinthians 13. The wife, in turn, responds not as a resentful and brutalized slave, but rather in cheerful submission to the one who is as concerned about her and her happiness as he is about himself. [17]

*Planning the wedding.* In our culture, planning a wedding is a major undertaking which involves decisions about flowers, attendants, dresses, photographers, the reception, the cake, the guest list and, for many, how all of this can be paid for. As a couple approaches the wedding day, the premarital counselor has three major responsibilities. First, he can encourage the participants to "take it easy" in their planning. Modern weddings are not only expensive, but they can also be so fatiguing that a couple is in a state of mental and physical exhaustion by the time they leave for the honeymoon. The counselor might have limited success encouraging couples and their families to proceed with caution, but without dampening enthusiasm he can still try to be somewhat of a modifying influence.

Second, the counselor must insure that the couple meet the legal requirements for marriage. This usually involves getting a license and having a blood test or other physical examination.

Third, the counselor—in this case the pastor—can go over the service in detail prior to the wedding. For most people their marriage ceremony is a climax to weeks of planning, but frequently the main participants are too tired or too emotionally "keyed up" to remember much of what is being said. It is important, therefore, that the service be discussed in detail beforehand in order that the meaning of the pastor's statements be understood, and that the spiritual aspects of the service be considered. If the couple are Christians they should realize that the wedding can be an important witness of their mutual commitment to Christ. For many this realization has an influence on the music that is selected and on other details of the service. If it can be done without too much distraction, a couple might also consider making a tape recording of the service since this can be very meaningful in the future.

## TECHNIQUES OF PREMARITAL COUNSELING

Whenever a church leader has the opportunity of speaking to a youth group about Christian marriage, dating or sex, he is involved in a form of premarital counseling. Most teenagers and single adults are vitally interested in their relationships with the opposite sex. As they date, these young people are forming attitudes about the other sex and learning how to relate to each other. In interacting with a young people's group the church leader is able to convey practical information, point to biblical teachings, and demonstrate values which can be helpful to the person who at this early time is formulating his views of marriage.

A second opportunity for premarital counseling comes with the establishing of discussion groups or classes for engaged couples. Such groups should not be too large (four or five couples is ideal) and should be limited to couples who have already decided to get married. Rather than making a dramatic public announcement of the group's beginning, which can lead to anxiety and apprehension on the part of the participants, the church leader might suggest to one or two engaged couples that possibly a group might be organized for those who are interested. As others hear of the idea by word of mouth, a group can be started.

At their first meeting, the participants might each give a thumbnail sketch about themselves and then discuss how the group will proceed. Ideally the format and subject matter should be flexible although it is wise to have at least some ground rules. Each couple should agree to come for as many meetings as possible, for example, and while discussion among the participants should be open and honest, the subject matter of the sessions might be kept confidential from those outside of the group. On a chalkboard or note pad, the group leader should jot down issues that the couples might want to discuss, and he may add a few suggestions of his own. The nature of communication, the meaning of love, the management of finances, the use of time, the question of in-laws, the importance of the honeymoon, the issues of sex and contraceptives, the control of sexual urges before marriage, the problems of pregnancy and childbirth, the ways of handling disagreements, the existence of doubts about marriage, the role of religion in the home, and the details of the biblical view of marriage, are among the topics that should be considered. On occasion a specialist—such as a financial adviser or gynecologist— might be invited to join the group for a session, and at other times it might be wise to have a married couple sit in. If the church leader is married, his spouse may be willing to become a regular part of the group. Obviously all of this will take time, perhaps eight or ten sessions.

Often it is meaningful to open each session in prayer, to limit the discussion to a given length of time (an hour and a half to two hours is maximum), to conclude with a period of prayer in which several people lead, to stop promptly on time, and then to have refreshments available for those who want to remain longer for fellowship and further discussion.

At the completion of a group counseling series, it is good to get suggestions from the participants concerning ways for improving future counseling. Often this feedback can be especially helpful if the group gets together several months after the couples have been married. Such an "alumni gathering" is a good opportunity for the newly married to discuss issues that they are now facing as husband and wife.

In spite of the opportunities for group discussion, most premarital counseling is of the individual type where the counselor meets alone with the couple and perhaps individually for a time or two with each of the two people involved. Even when a couple is participating in a group, some private sessions are worth arranging. Here again, the format should be flexible and, although a minimum of three sessions is recommended, there can be more if the counselor can schedule the time.

In their premarital sessions some counselors follow a prearranged formula: a session on rapport-building and discussion of the biblical view of marriage; a session on roles, responsibilities, personality differences, and potential problems in marriage; and a session discussing details of the ceremony. While such a guideline is acceptable and often very helpful, it should not be followed too rigidly. Sometimes a counselor may want to give the couple a copy of Table 3-2 with the suggestion that they complete it prior to the next session. We may first want to discover what the couple has discussed between themselves about marriage, and then to introduce other relevant topics. At times it is appropriate to loan a book with the suggestion that it be read prior to the next session.[18] In all of this the counselor should be understanding and try to keep the interview pleasant and nonthreatening. While most premarital counseling will be done with the couple together, at some time a personal interview with each person can be helpful. This enables the counselor to assess each individual's readiness for marriage and to guide in the self-evaluation discussed earlier in the chapter.[19]

SPECIAL PROBLEMS IN PREMARITAL COUNSELING

It would be convenient, although a lot less fun, if every couple who is contemplating marriage could be counseled in the same way. This, of course, is impossible since each couple presents characteristics which are in some sense unique. Some problems, including the following, are especially difficult to handle.[20]

*Parental disapproval of the marriage.* A pastor who knows

all of the participants is in a tight spot in this situation. All parties may have good stated reasons for their opinions, so the counselor becomes a mediator, trying to bring about a reconciliation. In such situations, time sometimes permits a cooling off, but this is by no means always true. If all parties involved can look at their own attitudes and motives (Are the couple rebelling? Are the parents afraid to let go? Are they disappointed that their child did not find a better choice?) and seek to communicate with each other, things would be better. Such an ideal is difficult to achieve, but it's worth trying.

It should be recognized, however, that this is one of those situations in which both sides might try to distort the counselor's words and try to "get him on our side." At times it may be appropriate to call all of the participants together and to clarify what your role will be in the situation.

*Premarital pregnancy.* This situation is frequently very stressful for all involved. When he learns of the situation, the counselor should encourage the couple to inform their parents, if this has not already been done, and to get proper medical attention. Feelings of shame, guilt and disappointment often must be dealt with over a long period of time, and the couple (and their parents) should be counseled as they decide what is their next course of action. Often a local physician can give helpful information on community agencies that minister specifically to unwed mothers. One thing, however, is certain. A shotgun marriage is not necessarily the best solution, for such marriages frequently end in bitterness and infidelity. The only time when marriage is advisable for a pregnant girl is when the conditions discussed earlier in this chapter would indicate that the marriage is likely to be successful in spite of the circumstances under which it begins. [21]

*Mixed marriages.* In the minds of many people, "mixed marriage" refers only to a union between persons of different races, but the term can be more broadly applied. When people of different religious, socioeconomic, educational, or age groups decide to marry, their relationship can also be described as "mixed." While many of these marriages succeed, an exceptionally large number develop serious problems. Differences in family background can lead to disagreements over values, interests and routine ways of living. Add to this the ostracism and disapproval from family and community residents, and the problems become especially difficult. If a couple are of "like precious faith" there is no scriptural reason why the color of their skin or the size of their bank account should prevent their getting married. In counseling with such couples, however, the church leader should make sure that they are fully aware of the difficulties involved, and he should assure them of his continued availability for counsel after the wedding.

*Mental illness.* Should severely disturbed people be permitted to marry? Sometimes this can be good therapy, but since a marriage can be no more stable than the individuals involved, the prospects for marital harmony in such cases are not very good. Normally the church leader should get the opinion of a qualified mental health professional before deciding whether or not to officiate at the marriage of a disturbed person. In the absence of such professional consultation it is probably best to be supportive but to encourage the couple to delay marriage until a more stable situation exists.

*Severe doubts.* Marriage is a lifelong commitment and because of its importance some couples approach it with real insecurity. It is common for couples to have periods of uncertainty as they approach their wedding day, and in such cases the feelings are best discussed openly and examined in light of the present reality. Usually it is wise to pray about these feelings, realizing that God leads in every aspect of life, including marriage.

Premarital anxiety is of two types.[22] *Common anxiety*

is a mild form of discomfort and uncertainty that is almost universal. The counselor can reassure such couples and help them to accept their feelings. *Panic*, as the term implies, is much more severe. It may occur a few hours before the wedding and lead the person involved to make irrational decisions, like wanting to elope or to cancel the wedding. The latter may be a wise alternative, although the counselor who has done a thorough job of premarital guidance will know if the wedding really should be held. If so, reassurance and the administering of mild sedation by a physician may help the individual meet the stressful marriage situation.

*Physical disability*. A physical handicap need not be a hindrance to marital happiness. The important thing is that the couple's attitudes toward it be discussed completely during the premarital counseling sessions. If there is genuine love accompanied by an understanding and acceptance of the disability, then marital success is quite possible.[23]

## MARITAL COUNSELING

Healthy marriage has been described by Clinebell as "at once the most demanding and the most potentially rewarding" of all human relationships.[24] As husband and wife, two adults merge their separate lives into an intimate and complex union which the Bible describes as good and honorable (Pr. 18:22; Heb. 13:4).

Mergers, however, are not always smooth. Often there are disagreement, distrust and misunderstanding before the two parties begin to function as a unit. The merger of two people in marriage can be likened to the coming together of two great rivers. For many miles the waters share the same riverbed, but only slowly is there a mixture so that the two become one. In most marriages this is a long, slow process. Some never achieve a mutually satisfying union, and for others the merger comes only when a counselor is present to guide.

As you read these words, hundreds of thousands of marriages—many probably in your own community—are sick and dying. Couples who went to the altar with high hopes and eager expectations have seen their marriages degenerate into tired friendship or a long drawn-out war. The reasons for this marital disharmony are both numerous and complex, but some of the more common include the following:

*Lack of communication.* Marriage counselors consistently report that couples who aren't getting along are often unable to communicate. [25] Sometimes there is open quarreling, sometimes sullen silence, but always there is inability to honestly share feelings and ideas about significant issues. While writing this chapter I met with a young couple who were on the verge of divorce. When they entered my office together, neither said much but both showed a lot of nonverbal hostility, mostly in the form of contemptuous glances at each other. Since we weren't getting far with them both in the room, I separated them and talked with each alone. When the spouse was absent, each spoke freely and gave the same message: "We can't talk about anything. All we do is shout and scream or give each other the silent treatment." To improve communication the partners must learn to transmit clear messages and to listen carefully. By patiently watching a couple as they interact, the counselor can often see where communication is breaking down; but to improve future interaction is a hefty assignment, especially when the couple doesn't particularly want to improve their communication.

*Immaturity.* Very often couples begin marriage with unrealistically high expectations, only to be disappointed and disenchanted when the relationship does not turn out as they had hoped. This realization can be cause for working harder at the marriage and making it a mutually satisfying experience. Planning new experiences together, having a cause for living, making opportunities for intimacy, ritual-izing romantic occasions, and continuing to spend time interacting with each other are ways that have been suggested for maintaining the relationship. [26]

For many couples, however, the disenchantment does not lead to increased efforts; instead, it encourages immature behavior that puts further strain on the marriage. Unreasonable demands, lack of consideration for the spouse's feelings, blaming the other for one's own faults, impulsive behavior, irresponsibility, intemperance, increased rigidity in one's attitudes, and an overdependency on the parents are all indications of immaturity.[27] Sometimes a person will develop an overdependence on the hoped-for intervention of God and refuse to work at the realities of the problems which exist. All of these attitudes take time to overcome. People don't mature in a day, and even with the understanding guidance of a counselor, a marriage built on immaturity will have a long slow road to improvement.

*Failure to take marriage seriously.* Several months ago an advertisement appeared in a psychological journal showing a young bride in her wedding dress. Underneath was the caption: "...till divorce do us part." It hasn't quite come to this yet, the advertisement proclaimed, "but almost as many marriages are ended by divorce as by death."

According to the Bible, marriage is a lifelong institution, but many people today fail to accept this view. They see marriage as an arrangement of convenience which lasts "for the forseeable future" and to be terminated at will by either or both of the parties involved. Even among married couples there may be many who feel no responsibility to remain faithful to their spouse. In one recent survey, for example, over 20,000 readers of *Psychology Today* magazine (most of whom are over 30 and well educated) answered questions about marriage and sex. Eighty percent of the respondents thought that extramarital sex was acceptable, and 40 percent of the men and 36 percent of the women had engaged in this behavior.[28] With this loose view of the sanctity of sex, and with divorce so widely accepted and so easily attained, there is less willingness for couples to work at a marriage and to insure its growth and survival. If things aren't going well, one can always get a divorce and find somebody better.*

Perhaps this attitude has developed because Western man has such a distorted view of love. Ask any couple why they plan to get married and the most common response is: "Because we are in love." If they later decide to get a divorce, one of the stated reasons is likely to be: "We don't love each other anymore." The Scriptures instruct husbands to love their wives (Eph. 5:25) and wives to love their husbands (Titus 2:4), but what does this mean? Popular ballads, poems and movies glorify love but the term is used so broadly that it is almost meaningless.

In regard to the marital relationship, the Bible gives two examples of what love should be like: First, husbands should love their wives as Christ loved the church (Eph. 5:25-27). The love of Christ is unselfish, and without strings attached. As described in 1 Corinthians 13, Christian love is patient, kind, and free of jealousy, envy, boasting, pride, grudges, rudeness or self-glorification. It is a giving relationship which involves loyalty and concern for the object of one's love. This kind of love cannot be "turned on" at will, nor is it something we "fall into or out of." Love is a growing relationship which, for Christians, is an outward expression of the love of Christ in a life. Marital love is also to be similar to self-love. Men should love their wives, the Scriptures say, as they love themselves (Eph. 5:28-33). This can hardly be consistent with the casual way in which some people view the marriage bond.

*This does not mean that all divorce is bad. Under some circumstances the Scriptures permit divorce (Deu. 24:1-4; Mt. 5:31-32; 19:3-10), but there is never endorsement of the idea that marriage is a casual and pragmatic arrangement to be prolonged if it works, and terminated if it doesn't.

*Unhealthy need fulfillment.* In any successful marriage, the participants will have certain needs fulfilled. The need for love, security, respect, acceptance, safety, and sexual fulfillment in marriage, for example, is so important, that one counselor has defined a happy marriage as "one in which there is a relatively high degree of mutual need satisfaction," and an unhappy marriage as one with much need frustration. [29] Sometimes marriages experience difficulty because one or both of the partners have needs that are not being met. In such cases, communication of the lack of fulfillment is important, and the partners can work—perhaps with the help of a counselor—to make the relationship more mutually need-satisfying.

In some marriages this is difficult to accomplish, especially if the normal needs are exaggerated to an excessive degree. When a person has an insatiable need to feel secure and be assured of acceptance; an intense desire to cling to or be dependent on someone else; a strong need to dominate, to hurt or to stand aloof; a perpetual urge for sex; or some similar intense desire, we conclude that his needs are neurotic and that the marriage is unhealthy. Improvement in such marriages is unlikely unless there is long-term counseling accompanied by patience and understanding on the part of the mate.

### THE GOALS OF MARRIAGE COUNSELING

In his contacts with married couples, the church leader can help in two important ways: he can guide in the building and improving of a marriage, and he can counsel with those who are having marital conflicts. Briefly stated, these are the two basic goals of marriage counseling. In both cases, the counselor is attempting to help the partners improve their relationships with each other and with God.

These two broad goals can be subdivided into more specific aims. The counselor should try, during the course of his counseling, to

92

—reopen lines of communication between the couple and to encourage the expression of feelings.

—encourage understanding of each person's own attitudes, goals, needs and views of marriage as well as those of one's spouse.

—help couples accept each other and stop trying to reform and transform each other.

—help the couple work together at translating their new understanding and acceptance into appropriate action so that the relationship is improved.

—interrupt the vicious cycle of mutual retaliation.

—be less demanding and more responsible in relating to each other.

—encourage commitment to Christ and a familiarity with the biblical guidelines for marital stability.

## THE TECHNIQUES OF MARITAL COUNSELING

Professional marriage counseling has become a complex specialty with a variety of techniques and several theoretical approaches.* While a detailed consideration of these is beyond the scope of this book, some guidelines can be used effectively by the sensitive church leader as he works with married couples.

---

*For information about the profession, contact Dr. William R. Reevy, Academy of Psychologists in Marital Counseling, Department of Psychology, New Mexico Institute of Mining and Technology, Socorro, N. M. 87801 or American Association of Marriage Counselors, 3603 Lemmon Avenue, Dallas, Tex. 75219. Some major theories of marriage counseling are summarized in B. L. Greene, *The Psychotherapies of Marital Disharmony.*

## COUNSELING THE NEWLY MARRIED

Even when there has been good premarital counseling, the first months and years of married life can be very demanding. During this time the young husband and wife are learning to adjust to each other and to their married status. Unanticipated conflicts, irritations, and communication breakdowns may frustrate the couple who, at least in the beginning, may have been expecting consistent marital bliss. It may be discovered that despite the careful planning before the wedding, it is not always easy to manage the money, get along smoothly with two sets of parents, or achieve a mutually satisfying sexual adjustment.[30]

Church leaders who recognize the value of premarital guidance sometimes fail to appreciate the importance of counseling after the honeymoon. If a couple can be guided during the early stages of married life, however, the marriage can be strengthened, and subsequent problems in the home can be avoided. But how does a church leader get started in counseling with newlyweds? Rarely does the couple come for counseling on their own, and they may be tired of hearing advice from well-meaning older people who have been married for a long time.

The value of counseling for the newly married should be stressed during the period of premarital counseling and perhaps at that time an appointment can be set up for sometime after the wedding. A pastoral call or two in the couple's new home gives the church leader a chance to visit the newlyweds and to ask, "How are things going now that you are married?" A Sunday school class for the newly married could provide opportunity for consideration of problem areas, or it might be helpful to establish an evening discussion group which would be attended by young couples during their first year of marriage. These get-togethers could each last for a couple of hours and could focus on issues which the group members identified as being important.[31] In all of this, the emphasis is not on giving advice but in helping young couples to understand themselves and their spouses better, and to work at building a more stable, satisfying marriage.

## JOINT AND INDIVIDUAL INTERVIEWS

Living together in the intimacies of marriage often leads to problems for which a couple needs help. When such marital difficulties arise, it is best for the husband and wife to both participate in the counseling, although there can be value in seeing only one spouse if the other absolutely refuses to cooperate or has no desire to continue the marriage.*

Whether the couple should be interviewed separately or in a joint session is a matter of debate among professional marriage counselors. When a couple is seen together, the counselor has an excellent chance to observe their relationship and to see how they communicate. If both sincerely want to get along better, there can be mutual discussion of the misunderstandings, disagreements, personality characteristics, and insensitivities that are undermining the marriage. But there can also be name-calling, insinuations, and attempts to outdo each other in impressing the counselor and deprecating the spouse. By seeing the husband and wife separately it is possible for the counselor to get a more accurate idea of what each is like and to see how each views the marriage with its problems. The counselee feels freer to talk and has less of a need to defend himself against the accusations of a hostile mate.

Because there is value in both joint and individual interviews, it is usually best to use a combination of both. While there can be no rigid rules about procedure, the

*Counseling with one spouse should permit emotional release as well as focus on how the counselee can change himself. The counselor should avoid taking sides, should recognize the likelihood of distortions in a one-sided account, and should not let the counseling sessions become only a time for criticizing the absent spouse (H. J. Clinebell, Jr., *Basic Types of Pastoral Counseling*).

couple might be seen together first, then individually, and later in joint sessions again. Even in the initial interview this combination can be helpful as an attempt is made to isolate the problem areas and to make plans for future counseling. Since there are likely to be disagreements and attempts to dominate when the couple are together, it is important that each be given equal opportunity to express an opinion. Questions which stimulate discussion (often of a heated type) and help to show areas of disagreement include the following:

Why aren't you getting along?

What kinds of problems do you have?

When did your problems begin?

How do you handle disagreements?

What don't you like about him (her)?

What do *you* do to make things worse?

What is good about your marriage now?

Why did you ever get married in the first place?

How do you think your marriage can be improved?

What do you expect from these counseling sessions?

As he works with the couple, the counselor must show concern, understanding, impartiality, and a willingness to listen. This does not mean that he just nods his head and says nothing. At times the counselor must ask for information, express his understanding, point out inconsistencies, answer questions, make reference to relevant biblical principles, give counsel, and confront the counselees with some of the ways in which they are contributing to the problem. At times it may be wise to refer a couple to a professional marriage counselor, and at other times the church leader may want to meet with several couples in group sessions. All of this implies that there be flexibility and openness on the part of the counselor, coupled with sensitivity and a willingness to be directive when this is necessary.

## SPECIAL AREAS OF MARITAL STRESS

While no two problem marriages have exactly the same weaknesses, the counselor encounters some issues time and time again.

*Role conflicts.* When a couple gets married they each have expectations of what a husband and wife are supposed to do in the marriage. These expectations arise largely from observations of how one's own parents functioned in *their* relationships. Almost everyone in our society expects that the husband will mow the lawn and the wife will prepare the meals, but there are other issues about which the couple may disagree. Who takes out the garbage, for example? Who plans the vacations, pays the bills, carves the Thanksgiving turkey, or changes diapers? The husband may think these are all a part of the wife's duties, but she may disagree. Conflicts arise almost invariably if the wife and husband think differently about whether married women should work, whether a working woman's money is hers to keep, whether a couple should visit his parents every Christmas, or whether a father should accompany his family to church. In a time and culture in which traditional family roles are changing, the husband and wife must expect to have different views of the position of each in the home. Instead of trying to mold and reform the other, however, each of the partners should be willing to discuss their divergent expectations—with a counselor's help if necessary—and seek to arrive at mutually acceptable compromises. Inability to do this is apparently a contributing factor to many divorces.[32]

*Money.* The love of money, according to the Scriptures, is the root of all evil (1 Tim. 6:10). Lack of money and disagreements about its use, according to several research reports, are the most common issues of conflict between husbands and wives.[33] The high cost of living, changing views of what are necessities, and "easy" installment buying are among the issues which lead families to overspend or to disagree on how the money should be distributed. Sometimes the conflicts are accentuated by a spouse who is a miser, a compulsive spender, or a poor planner in the use of money.[34]

Careful planning can prevent or at least reduce many of the financial problems of marriage. How the money is to be spent will depend somewhat on necessities (taxes are inevitable), somewhat on values (some people value stylish clothes, others would rather spend money on a vacation), and to a large extent on the size of one's income. When couples have different ideas on how to spend money, the use of a wife's income, or the value of installment purchases, there must be more discussion and compromise—sometimes with a counselor's help.

*In-laws.* When a man marries, he leaves his father and mother and cleaves to his wife (Mt. 19:5). Presumably the wife makes a similar break from her parents when she submits herself to her husband (Eph. 5:22). In practice, of course, this transition is not nearly so precise. Instead, we talk about "marrying into a family," and as everybody knows, when a person takes a spouse, he or she also collects a whole new group of relatives.

Relationships with relatives can be consistently smooth and pleasant, especially if everyone works at building the family rapport. But this doesn't always happen. As the many jokes about in-laws would imply, it is not always easy for a couple to deal with the relatives and vice-versa. Parents are sometimes overpossessive, overdomineering or disapproving of the marriage. Married "children" are some-

98

times overdependent, rebellious, or critical of the parents. The problems are especially acute if the husband and wife are of different educational, class, ethnic, or religious background.

In marital counseling the attitudes of in-laws and attitudes toward in-laws should be discussed. These in-law problems sometimes are the major cause of disagreement, while at other times they lurk in the background, indirectly influencing other problems.[35] The opinions of in-laws, for example, may have a great effect on a couple's disagreements over money or appropriate husband-wife roles. As with other interpersonal conflicts, counselees should be helped to express feelings which may have been dormant, to understand the other person's perspective, and to work at improving the strained relationships. Sometimes it is necessary to accept the inevitability of a difficult in-law situation and to live with it as peacefully as we can (Ro. 12:18).

*Sex.* Sexual intercourse should be the highest expression of love between a man and a woman. Here two people cleave as "one flesh" wholly committed to each other in physical and psychological union.

For many couples this is a reality, but for others it is a fictional idea. Frigidity, impotency, inability to experience orgasm at the same time, infidelity, disagreements over the use of contraceptives, differences in sexual desires, insensitivity to each other's feelings, and a number of other problems may prevent real sexual fulfillment in a marriage.

It should be emphasized that sex often gets blamed as a *cause* for marital difficulties when really it is a *symptom* of some other problem. Certainly there is no one-to-one relationship between marital instability and sexual problems, but more often than not, prolonged sexual problems reflect other kinds of difficulties between the husband and wife. Marital problems are not "solved in bed." Instead, they are reflected in the couple's sex life. In such cases the counseling should focus not so much on the symptom (sex) as on the other issues that are causing friction between a couple. When a couple is really working at their relationship and making progress in getting along, their sexual problems can be solved. Consultation with a physician, discussion with a more experienced married couple, reading a book on sex, and freely discussing feelings and frustrations with each other, all are ways in which a couple can improve the sex act if they both want a change for the better.

*Pregnancy and childbirth.* A couple may experience mixed feelings when they learn that the wife is pregnant for the first time. There is often excitement at the prospect of parenthood, accompanied by a realization that one's style of life will soon change. If the couple have been active in doing things together, if the wife has had a good job, or if children were not wanted at this time, the early months of pregnancy can be especially difficult. For all couples parenthood involves taking on new roles, new routines, and perhaps a lowered standard of living as the wife's income stops and the presence of a third person in the home increases expenses. The wife's physical condition may have a psychological influence so that she has periods of discouragement and weeping. All of this can put a strain on a marriage—especially an unstable one—but communication of feelings between the couple and a willingness to understand each other can make pregnancy and the beginning of parenthood a rewarding experience.

The same kind of mutual concern should be present when a couple wants children but the wife cannot get pregnant. Often the church leader can encourage and support such couples as they seek medical consultation or as they go through the long and frustrating procedures that are required for those who choose to adopt a baby.

*Spiritual conflicts.* Research studies show that families who pray and worship together do, indeed, stay together and have a much lower divorce rate than nonreligious families. But religion contributes to marital stability only insofar as it is shared by both husband and wife.[36] There are likely to be conflicts, for example, if one is deeply religious or committed to the lordship of Christ while the other is a nonbeliever or less committed. The apostle Paul advised such couples to stay together (1 Co. 7:12-13), but it is to be expected that in such situations there will be differences in values, preferences for leisure activities, standards for raising children, amount of participation in church services, and interest in other religious activities.

In these marriages the believer should pray for the spouse, seek to lead him to a commitment to Christ, and do what one can to maintain marital stability, providing this does not conflict with the guidelines of Scripture. The church leader can encourage the believer, befriend and witness to the unbeliever, and pray for both.

THE PROBLEM OF DIVORCE

In spite of the best efforts of the counselor and the parties involved, many marriages do fail. When this happens, couples are faced with three alternatives. They can "stick it out," grimly residing in the same house but with no real interest in each other and often with considerable conflict. Second, there can be separation in which the couple lives apart but without the freedom to remarry, and third, there can be divorce—the complete dissolution of the marriage with the freedom to remarry.[37]

Legally there can be numerous grounds for divorce, with the laws differing from place to place. In contrast, the Bible has a more stringent set of requirements and appears to give only two grounds for divorce for the Christian: desertion by an unbeliever (1 Co. 7:15) and adultery (Mt. 5:32; 19:9; Lk. 16:18).

While the counselor will want to do everything in his power to heal broken marriages, he must realize that at times separation or divorce is unavoidable and may be the best solution for all involved. When this happens there are likely to be considerable adjustment problems. There are often feelings of loneliness, hostility, insecurity, guilt, rejection, and loss of self-esteem. There are difficulties adjusting to the role of "divorced person" and a concern about the welfare of the children who now are from a broken home. In many cases, a stable one-parent family may be superior to a two-parent family that is torn by marital strife, but the absence of one parent from the home can also cause difficulties, especially for young children.

When a marriage is breaking up and there seems to be no hope for reconciliation, the church must not abandon the couple. The pastor can give encouragement, guidance, and supportive counseling to the participants— helping them to adjust to the stresses and to face the reality of a marriage failure. He can also encourage church members to be accepting. Too often we treat the divorced person like a second-class citizen who is beyond forgiveness. But even when sin *is* clearly involved in the divorce, we must recognize that God forgives (1 Jn. 1:9) and the follower of Christ must do likewise.

## FAMILY COUNSELING

We live in a period when the family is changing drastically. No longer the tightly knit unit that it once was, the family is, in the opinion of some, becoming less and less important in our culture. While this analysis may be true in many respects, the family still fulfills some unique and crucial roles in Western society. It is the accepted channel for childbirth; it provides shelter and protection; it educates, especially in the early years; it largely determines one's status in life; it gives religious instruction and determines whether or not a child will be in contact with the church; it guides in recreational activities; and it provides the love and affection which are necessary for survival and development. Families differ in the efficiency with which they do all of this, and they differ in the ability of the members to get along with one another. But in spite of its problems and changes, the family is still a core part of the society.

The many problems of the modern family have been summarized and analyzed in a number of books and articles. The birth of a deformed or unwanted child, the delinquency of a teenager, the demands of an aging parent, the death of a loved one, the "empty nest" when the last child gets married, the serious illness of a family member, the loss of family income—these and other events put stress on the family and demand some kind of readjustment. This becomes especially difficult when family members are unable to communicate, cannot agree on values, or lack respect for one another.

To deal with problems such as these, counselors traditionally worked with individual family members. Over the years, however, it became more and more apparent that something more was needed because the value of individual counseling was often undermined when the counselee went back into the turmoil of a family in conflict. To meet this problem, some counselors began to work with the family as a group.[38] In counseling, the family members (of school age and above) meet together to discuss their mutual problems, to increase mutual understanding, and to learn how to improve communication.

The church leader may find himself involved in a simple form of family counseling whenever he makes a pastoral call. In more formal counseling the family might come to the church to meet together with the counselor. In this situation it is sometimes good to talk briefly with the parents alone, and briefly with the children alone, but most of the time should be spent with the whole family meeting together.[39] Each family member should be given the opportunity to talk about the family problems from his perspective. At first this is likely to be threatening to the participants, but as the counselor encourages openness and is himself a model of good communication, the discussion becomes freer. As with all pastoral counseling, the group leader may suggest that the family should consider one or two relevant Bible passages, and there is value in encouraging prayer together. Thus, family counseling becomes a special form of the group counseling discussed in chapter 2.

## SUMMARY

In a study conducted several years ago, college men and women were asked what they expected would bring the greatest satisfaction in life. Sixty percent of the men and 87 percent of the women replied, "Family relations." Apparently most young people in our society look forward to marriage and a family of their own, although many are later disappointed. The problems of marriage lead one out of three couples to get a divorce, and numerous others live together in frustration and family misery.

In his counseling, the church leader will likely spend more time dealing with marriage and family problems than with any other issue. Before marriage, couples should be guided in their preparation for life together. After the wedding, newlyweds can be helped in their adjustments to marriage and subsequent parenthood. When problems arise, the church leader can work to heal broken relationships and stimulate better communication between the husband, wife and other members of the family. All of this takes time, effort and skill, but the end result can be family units which function smoothly and are committed to following and serving Jesus Christ.

# 4
## Vocational Counseling

Choosing a vocation is one of man's most significant and far-reaching decisions. Our choice of occupation determines how we will spend at least one-third of our waking hours, for this is the minimum amount of time that most people spend at work during their adult lives. Our work determines our income and this, in turn, affects one's standard of living and place of residence. The kind of work that we do and the success of our careers have an influence on the type of people we have for friends, on our status in the community, on the kind of relationships we have with our families (the homelife of a busy pastor will likely be very different from that of an office worker or traveling salesman), on our general satisfaction with life (it is hard to be really happy if you hate your job), and on our emotional well-being and feelings of self-worth. Even the church that a person attends is related to his work. There are exceptions, of course, but studies have shown that business executives and professional people tend to affiliate with Episcopalian and Presbyterian churches, farmers and manual workers tend to be Methodists, while the Baptist church is frequently the choice of "workingmen." [1]

The selection of an occupation has added importance for the Christian. When we acknowledge that Christ is Lord, we must turn over our whole lives—including our working lives—to His control. It becomes crucial, then, that our choice of an occupation be in accordance with divine will, and that our daily work be done diligently "as unto Christ" (Eph. 6:5-6).

In view of the social, psychological and theological importance of work, the choice of a vocation should be made with great care and deliberation. Too often, however, the decision is made in a haphazard and hurried fashion. Parents, teachers, friends, and others in our society expect occupational decisions to be made early. Thus, at a time when they are inexperienced, idealistic, and struggling with the problems of adolescence, young people have the added responsibility of choosing from an almost unlimited number of career possibilities. Is it surprising that so many end up dissatisfied and frustrated with their jobs? For perhaps vast numbers of people, work does not offer any challenge but is, instead, a boring drugery which must be endured—for life.

To help people avoid this unhappy situation and make wise occupational choices, vocational guidance counseling has become more and more prominent within recent years. Industries, governmental agencies, private employment organizations, and schools have hired specialists who are trained to help individuals choose, prepare for, embark on, and adjust to an occupation. These vocational counselors are thoroughly familiar with the occupational world and have the ability to administer and interpret psychological tests, the results of which can be of great help to the job seeker. Rarely, however, do professional people consider the will of God in one's choice of work. It is here that the church leader can play a special role. He cooperates with the professional vocational counselor, but adds a dimension which is uniquely Christian. His concern extends not only to those who are trying to choose a vocation, but also to those who are frustrated in their jobs, or struggling with decisions about education, or for some reason unable to work, or facing the boredom of retirement.

# Vocational Counseling Techniques

Whenever one person talks with another about a career choice, vocational counseling is, to some extent, taking place. Whether the counseling is of this informal nature or more professional in character, it involves three basic aspects: being familiar with the world of work, knowing the counselee, and guiding in the making of decisions.

## KNOWING THE WORLD OF WORK

What would you really like to accomplish in your life work? If you ask this question, people usually give one or more of the following answers: "to help people," "to get personal success in terms of money or fame," or "to express myself in some way" (as in writing or art).[2] To achieve goals such as these, a lot of people apparently think that they must enter a profession. This is highly unrealistic and for many will lead to severe disappointment. In one survey, for example, it was found that 80 percent of high school counselees had been encouraged by their counselors (and probably by their parents) to prepare for a professional career. However, qualifications for a profession are high, and only about 20 percent of teenagers can eventually be accommodated by the professions, so it is clear that 60 percent had overly high aspirations and eventually were forced to lower their sights and enter less prestigious positions.[3]

This kind of disappointment can be prevented if the counselor knows something about the world of work and the requirements for various occupations. But this is not an easy task. Literally thousands of job opportunities are available, and even the professional guidance counselor cannot keep fully abreast of all developments in the field. How, then, can the pastor, Sunday school teacher, or other church leader help the occupation seeker? The answer is twofold: show him where to get information, and suggest the questions that he should ask about different jobs.

*Sources of information.* Two of the best places to get occupational information are in the school guidance office and the local library. Frequently these places contain occupational information files, books describing various vocations, catalogs and brochures describing training or educational opportunities, and relevant government publications. In the United States, for example, the government produces several helpful publications, including the *Occupational Outlook Handbook*, the *Occupational Guides* and the *Dictionary of Occupational Titles*. The latter, usually referred to as the DOT, is the most complete source of information. Published in several volumes, it is a massive compilation which describes thousands of jobs and categorizes them into seven major occupational groupings:

professional and managerial occupations

clerical and sales occupations

service occupations

agricultural, fishery, forestry and kindred occupations

skilled occupations

semiskilled occupations

unskilled occupations

A second source of information is the people who live in the community who are willing to talk about their work. A good way to learn about the insurance business, for example, is to talk with an insurance salesman. While such interviews can be helpful, they are time-consuming and limited by the availability of resource people.

Third, information is often available from trade unions

and professional organizations. When someone asks me for information about the profession of psychology, for example, I usually suggest that they write to the American Psychological Association and request a booklet entitled *A Career in Psychology.*\* Many other organizations provide similar occupational literature.

*Type of information.* When one has located the depository of information, what sort of things does he look for as he tries to find out about jobs? This will vary from situation to situation. Some occupations are rare or obscure and we need to ferret out a great deal of information. Other fields of work are well known and the counselee may only want to uncover one or two pertinent facts. In either case, Table 4-1 can be a helpful guideline.

If some member of the church is interested in vocational guidance, we can perform a useful service by telling him where vocational information is available, giving him a copy of Table 4-1 as a guide in his information search, and then meeting with him to discuss his findings. This collection of information is only a part of vocational guidance, but it can be a significant and important part.

## KNOWING THE COUNSELEE

There are many reasons why people choose to enter a specific occupation. The opinions of parents are very important—especially with younger people—but in addition there are the influence of friends or teachers, the interest that comes from hobbies and extracurricular activities, the glamour and prestige that are associated with different occupations (being a surgeon sounds much more attractive than being a used-car salesman), the information that describes various careers, and the student's evaluation of his own abilities and potentialities.

\*Write American Psychological Association, 1200 Seventeenth Street, N.W., Washington, D. C. 20036 for the booklet by C. A. Boneau et al., *A Career in Psychology.*

# Table 4-1

## Occupational Information*

In seeking information about a vocation, the following questions should be asked:

1. What is the nature of the work?
    How does a person in this occupation spend his time?
    What tasks does he perform?

2. What training is required?
    What are the educational requirements?
    Where does one get training?
    How long will it take?
    How much does it cost?

3. What personal qualifications are needed?
    Does it require certain abilities, special skills, or physical requirements?

4. Who can enter the occupation?
    Are there restrictions in terms of sex, race, age, citizenship, or religion?
    Is it necessary to belong to a union or religious group?
    Are special examinations required for this occupation—such as licensing, ordination, or acceptance into a union?

5. What are the working conditions?
    What are my surroundings?
    Do I work indoors or out?
    What are the hours?
    With whom do I work?
    Are there seasonal variations in the work?
    To whom will I be responsible?

6. What is the remuneration?
    What is the average income?
    What is the range of income?
    What are the fringe benefits in terms of housing, allowances, bonuses, retirement plans, medical expenses, extra fees, etc.?

7. What are the personal satisfactions of this work?
    What is its status in the community?
    What are its strong and weak points?
    Is it interesting?
    Would it be personally fulfilling?

8. How will it influence my personal life?
    Will it influence my family?
    Will it require me to compromise any moral principles?
    Will it keep me in one geographical location?
    Will it require a great deal of traveling?

9. What is its potential for the future?
    Will jobs be available in the future?
    Will it be overcrowded (or is it now)?
    Is it likely to fade out in the future?
    As I get older will I still be able to stay in this job?
    If not, does it pave the way for something I *can* do?

10. How does this fit with one's desire to serve Christ?
    Can a Christian honestly pursue this line of work?
    Is it a wise use of my God-given abilities?
    As far as I can determine, is this consistent with God's will for my life?

*Adapted from C. F. Kemp, *The Pastor and Vocational Counseling;* and M. F. Baer and E. S. Roeber, *Occupational Information: The Dynamics of Its Nature and Use.*

One of the guidance counselor's biggest tasks is to help the counselee get a more realistic appraisal of himself. The professional vocational counselor would probably conduct an interview and give a number of tests in order to get this information. But even without skills in psychological testing, the church leader can help the counselee to evaluate himself in the following areas:

*General ability.* A lot of people may want to be physicians but not many people are smart enough to handle the rigorous requirements of medical school. In vocational counseling we must try to help the counselee set his aspirations in accordance with his ability. Usually this will involve slowing down someone whose goals are unrealistically high, but occasionally we must encourage capable people who have set their sights too low. The student's grades are often a good indication of his ability and of his potential for performance in later schooling.

*Specific abilities.* Most of us have special abilities in at least one or two areas and these should be considered in vocational planning. Some people, for example, are mechanically inclined—they can fix anything. Others have unusual musical ability or a special way of getting along with people. Equally important are a person's noticeable weaknesses. A person who can't throw a ball obviously would be ill-advised if we encouraged a career in baseball.

*Personality traits.* People with equal intellectual ability are not equally suited for the same occupations. Some are shy and withdrawn; others are outgoing. Some like a lot of change; others prefer life to be more orderly and routine. Some are cheerful, impulsive, active or critical, while others might be less cheerful, prone to plan carefully, and more lethargic and accepting. Personality differences such as these are very important in vocational choice and adjustment. The person who wants to be a missionary had better be flexible, accepting and able to get along with people, for example, or he is heading for trouble.

*Interests.* Our likes and dislikes are also important in career choice. While tests give a good summary of such interests, it can also be helpful to reflect on our preferences and jot these down on a piece of paper. As a start, we might ask how we spend our spare time and money. This is an excellent barometer of one's values and gives a good clue to one's interests. It should be emphasized that the counselee should try to identify his own real interests and not simply reflect on the suggestions and aspirations of his parents or teachers.

*Spiritual state.* The person who is deeply committed to Christ and wanting to serve Him in all aspects of life, will approach vocational counseling with different aspirations than will the non-Christian or the halfhearted believer. The Christian counselor would certainly want to ascertain the counselee's spiritual state, therefore, and at some time discuss the believer's responsibility to spend his life in service to Christ and in the place of His choosing.

*Other factors.* Certain occupations are closed to people on the basis of sex, age, physique, health, lack of training or other similar issues. In spite of civil rights legislation, color of skin still seems to be a barrier to success in some occupations and, in others, citizenship is a deterrent. In some states, for example, a non-American cannot get a license to teach or practice his profession—regardless of his competence or quality and place of training. In most denominations, women cannot be ordained as ministers; and no mission society will accept candidates who are physically unhealthy. Individual differences such as these *must* be considered in vocational planning.

GUIDING IN THE DECISION PROCESS

It would be convenient if the counselor could analyze the world of work, appraise the counselee's characteristics, and then announce the one perfect occupation. Such a goal is, of course, impossible. Even if we could attain complete knowledge of the job market and of an individual's traits, it is unlikely that we would come up with one "perfect job." For most people several occupations could be satisfying, but none is likely to be perfect in all respects.

The work of the counselor, therefore, is to help the counselee acquire the needed information and to guide as he uses this to make his vocational decision. In the words of one writer,

> ...we need to help young people learn how to make decisions which are, on the one hand, appropriate for them, and on the other hand, realistic and flexible. This means that they need to know what alternative courses of action are open to them; what the consequences and risks of choosing each of them are; and how these factors relate to their own system of values. They need to become aware that the ultimate responsibility for making choices rests with them, but that we stand ready to help them in the decision making process....We need to (and indeed must) "motivate" adolescents to make the choices, educationally and vocationally, which are feasible for them at their stage of development.[4]

## Special Issues in Vocational Counseling

Guiding a young person in his choice of a career may be the vocational counselor's most frequent task, but it should not be his only responsibility. Many people are already in the labor force but are dissatisfied. Others are frustrated because they are out of work and unable to find employment. What can the counselor and especially the church leader do to help these unhappy people? In answer, consider five special vocation counseling situations:

### THE UNEMPLOYED

The church is not an employment agency, but at times the pastor or other church members encounter someone who is out of work and in need of guidance in finding a job. In ministering to such people our first task is to express a sincere concern. Since it is often frustrating and discouraging to be unemployed, the church leader performs a real service by being a sympathetic listener, by reminding the counselee of God's care and concern, and by praying with the job seeker. This is not to imply that a short sermon and a prayer provide the solution to the problem and relieve the counselor of any further responsibility. The book of James warns against such a simplistic approach to the needy (2:14-17). However, if the unemployed person and his friend in the church can consider the situation *together* and can pray together, this can be a significant step in the right direction.

In an age of welfare checks and unemployment insurance, it is often easy to forget that the unemployed person might also be in need of practical assistance. Depending somewhat on the length of time that one has been unemployed, it might be helpful if the church could provide clothing, food, or other tangible help. In our society such help is often embarrassing to the recipient and a threat to his self-esteem. Because of this the church leader should be careful to insure that the gift is given in a way that is minimally embarrassing.

The church leader, especially the pastor, is rarely in a position to know of available employment opportunities in the community. In spite of this, he can make suggestions, such as the following, which might help the job seeker find work:

Use all available sources of information, including government job listings, college or private placement bureaus, classified advertisements, friends and relatives, etc.

Apply at a number of places. It never hurts to have an application on file in several personnel offices.

Have references lined up. Before looking for a job, know whom you will list as references, and get their prior permission.

Prepare a mimeographed biographical outline. This should include pertinent information such as one's age, education, past experience, previous employment, names of references, etc. The outline should be carefully prepared, neatly typed, and used in letters to prospective employers or as a supplement to application forms.

Try not to get discouraged. Finding a job is often a long, time-consuming process, and personnel decisions are not made quickly.

For job interviews, dress appropriately, be relaxed and do not try too hard to impress. Be yourself and be honest. [5]

## THE DISSATISFIED

Several years ago a psychologist named Donald Super wrote an influential book on the psychology of careers. According to Super, there are five stages of vocational development. The *growth stage*, which extends from conception to about age fourteen, is a time of occupational fantasy. The child does not have to make realistic work choices but can move ahead on the assumption that when he grows up he can "be anything" he wants. In a world of imagination he can pretend that he is a potential cowboy, a fireman, or—if he is a Canadian—a Mounty.

The ages between about fifteen and twenty-five are labeled the *exploratory stage*. Here the person is trying to "find himself," to develop his values, and to make realistic occupational plans. He will probably select—and discard—a number of occupations before settling on one area of work. During this stage he must learn how to find a job and how to cope with the problems of adjusting to the routines and requirements of work. He often learns that promotions are slow in coming, that salaries are lower than he expected, and that there is a big gap between where he is and where he would like to be. There is considerable aimlessness and mobility during this stage as the young person flounders in trying to find a suitable vocational niche.

This is followed by the *establishment stage* during which the worker establishes a family, a home, and a place in the community. There may be mobility during this stage, but there is less floundering. The person has found a place in the world of work and is now attempting to establish himself. Super suggests that this stage begins at about age twenty-five and lasts until one is in the mid-forties. For some people, however, including those who must go through a long period of education, it is probable that the establishment stage begins and ends later. It is during this period, as people are struggling to establish themselves, that the most significant and lasting contributions to society are made.

During the *maintenance stage* the individual seeks to "hold his own." Having made a place in the vocational world, he now seeks to continue his level of efficiency until the time of retirement. Although there are exceptions, most people in this period of life make no attempt to be boldly creative or to try something new. If a person has reached his life goals, this can be a time of real satisfaction. It can also be a time of frustration for the individual who didn't achieve as he had hoped and who realizes that he will be forced to lower his aspirations.

When he reaches the age of retirement, the person enters the stage of *decline.* This involves a tapering off in one's vocational activities and an adjustment to retirement.

In any of these stages, with the exception of the first, people may be dissatisfied with their careers. During the exploratory stage there will be floundering and frustration, but there is also hope. Eventually, the young person believes, he will find a position which is satisfying and fulfilling. As they move into the establishment and maintenance stages, however, many people are forced to face hard reality. Bischof says these adult years are "a time of truth" when the dreams and aspirations of the twenties, thirties and early forties must give way to the reality of the present.[6] People discover that they are not succeeding as they had hoped and that they will not advance much beyond their present position. Many feel "locked in" to a dissatisfying job situation with no alternative but to wait it out until retirement. When faced with this truth, people respond in one or both of two ways. They may make up for the lack of occupational success by trying to succeed elsewhere—such as in church work, service clubs, lodges, or on the golf course—or they can rationalize, finding real or imagined reasons to explain why they didn't make it.

The church leader can help the dissatisfied worker in several ways. Once again, he can express concern and be a sympathetic listener, but as he considers the situation with the counselee, it might also be wise to discuss some practical alternatives. There are at least six of these, according to Dickerson: [7]

*Start a new occupation.* Although many men do succeed in changing jobs in middle age, this is not easy. The job change is often accompanied by a lowering of salary, a loss of seniority and fringe benefits, and perhaps a need to return to school for more training. For men with families, all of this can create a very heavy burden. For those who decide to move anyhow, there is the discovery that employers prefer to hire younger men in spite of laws which are designed to prevent discrimination against older workers.*

The worker who is determined to change his occupation should be alerted to these and other problems. In addition, the counselee might be advised to consider the alternatives which are listed below and to talk with a professional vocational guidance counselor before a change is initiated.

*Change employers.* In some occupations this is quite common and acceptable. The individual stays in the same occupation, so his experience counts, but he moves to another employer. Pastors do this frequently and so do college professors—often with an accompanying advance in salary. Many salesmen periodically change companies, hoping thereby to find a better product or a higher rate of

*In the United States, the Age Discrimination in Employment Act became law in 1967.

commission. For some occupations, however, this is a drastic move, involving a drop in salary and a loss of fringe benefits or seniority. Therefore, before making such a move in middle life, the possible consequences should be carefully considered.

*Change jobs within the same company.* This permits a man to retain his seniority and salary but to find working conditions or associates which are more to his liking. In some professional situations it is possible to alter one's duties in order to make over the job in accordance with one's preferences. Ministers, for example, might be able to emphasize some special part of their ministry—such as sermon preparation or counseling—and leave some of their remaining duties to others.

*Stay in the present job.* At times this may be the most feasible alternative—to stay with the problem job and to get satisfactions elsewhere. For the layman, the church is one place where there can be opportunities for rewarding and meaningful Christian service.

*Change oneself.* Might it be that the problem is not so much with the work as it is with the worker? Perhaps a critical attitude, an unwillingness to cooperate, a festering resentment, an inability to accept authority, or a severe disappointment with one's job may make the situation seem worse than it really is. Sometimes difficulties in the home or disturbing personal problems come out at work. In all of these cases the worker could benefit from self-examination accompanied by the counsel of a church leader or professional psychologist.

*Change one's attitude toward work.* Sometimes Christians have the idea that unless they are in a full-time church-related occupation they are not really serving God. In certain circles, the missionary is considered to be most in God's will, followed in turn by the pastor, other full-time workers, and then "those who have compromised with the world." The Bible gives no support to this thinking. Indeed, while

118

many occupations are mentioned in Scripture, there is never a suggestion that one is better than another.[8] As Christians we must diligently serve Christ in everything that we do, including work. In our secular jobs we should serve our employers as faithfully as if we were working directly for Christ (Eph. 6:5-8).

The dignity of work well done is perhaps a value which is fading from our society. We must remember, however, that a Christian is a witness wherever he goes. This is not to imply that we should be talking to people about Christ when an employer is paying him to do something else, for that kind of witnessing is really stealing. But the Christian should be as good an employee as possible, reflecting the power of Christ in his life. These kinds of witnesses are needed in every area of work, including the places which are not very glamorous or otherwise rewarding.

## THE SENIOR CITIZEN

In our complex, changing technological society, with its adulation of youth, there is little place for the person who is in the stage of decline. In government and industry, sixty-five is the compulsory age of retirement, and at that point a person is "pensioned off," regardless of his abilities or desire to continue working.

In an earlier volume in this Psychology for Church Leaders series we have discussed some of the frustrations faced as people approach and cope with retirement.[9] Here we limit our consideration to the practical ways in which older people can be helped vocationally. As he reaches and enters the time of retirement, the so-called senior citizen has three overlapping alternatives. He can prepare for and learn to adjust to retirement, he can find new work, and/or he can find some kind of substitutes for his work.

*Coping with retirement.* In spite of popular notions about the "golden years," few people approach retirement enthusiastically.[10] While the prospect of freedom from work is attractive, many people fear that they will lose status, self-respect, and the companionship of co-workers when they retire. The end of one's working career almost always means a reduction of income and a corresponding decline in one's standard of living. Hobbies which were once pursued so actively tend to lose their attraction, and it is well known that, for many, retirement is a time of aimless boredom and searching for something to do.[11] Even the freedom from one's lifelong routine can be a problem, and together these problems sometimes lead a person to be severely depressed.[12]

Happily, many industries and businesses are now helping their employees to prepare for and adjust to retirement. Some are able to arrange for a tapering-off period in which the employee works less and less, rather than quitting abruptly. Preretirement counseling and discussion groups, along with clubs for retired employees, can also make the transition easier. Research shows that adjustment is smoother when people have an accurate picture of what retirement will be like and when they can discuss their fears beforehand so that they are able to develop a positive attitude toward retirement.[13] This is a place where the church leader can make a valuable contribution. Through individual counseling and discussions with others who are retired or approaching retirement, the older person can be helped to a smoother transition out of the labor force.

*Finding new work.* There is nothing about age sixty-five that makes one old. Many people are both able and willing to work after their retirement, but the problem comes in finding jobs. Although research has clearly shown otherwise, some employers still believe that the older worker is more accident prone, less productive, and more likely to leave the firm than are younger employees.[14] Even the older person's rigidity and inability to learn have been called into question. With advancing years it may take longer to learn, but it can still be done. Another problem that faces employers is the aspirations of younger employees who want the company's top ranks thinned out so that there will be opportunity for advancement. Also, if an older person is injured, we know that his recovery will be longer and more expensive. For this reason the hiring of older workers may adversely influence the employer's insurance rates.

In spite of these obstacles, jobs *are* available for older people—especially part-time jobs—and government or private employment agencies know about these positions. The pastoral counselor can encourage older people in their search for work and can be alert to employment opportunities for which an older person might be suited. As employers are now being encouraged to hire parolees, the handicapped, and former mental patients, we might also encourage the hiring of older workers when this is possible.

*Finding substitute activities.* Many opportunities are available for older people who are willing to work on a volunteer basis in the church or community. The church leader can make these needs known and can encourage the retired person to keep active.

The problem is that older people, while willing to serve gratis, often need money. For this reason the church and other parts of society might consider ways in which people can receive at least a small honorarium for their volunteer work. This may be a wise expenditure of the Lord's money.

## THE MARRIED WOMAN

Several years ago, before the Women's Liberation movement began to gather momentum, a Pulitzer Prize-winning poet named Phyllis McGinley wrote a delightful little book in which she extolled the joys of being a housewife and mother:

> Because we are so many, we are sometimes downgraded in our own eyes. We form no unions, belong to no professional organizations. We do not federate, lobby in the Senate, go

on strike, scream for shorter working days, or establish corporations. Our hours are peculiar, our wages irregular. Few honors come to us in the shape of scrolls or Doctorates or Chairmanships of Foundations named with our names. If we have any public status apart from that which our husbands' abilities bring us, it is limited and local....The Nobel Committee has yet to award any laurels to a woman simply for making her home a place of such peace and delight that her family might rightfully rise up and call her blessed—if such an odd notion ever occurred to them.

Nevertheless, ours is a true profession, ancient, honorable, and unique. Compared to it, all other careers are upstarts.... Whether one likes or loathes the daily round of chores, whether one personally wields a broom or leaves it to apter talents, has no bearing on my premise—that it is into the hands of women life has dropped its most significant duties. [15]

In spite of the joys of being a homemaker, a woman's work is difficult and frequently unappreciated. For the housewife who has a good education and has enjoyed a short career in nursing, teaching, office work or some other field, the role of changing diapers, mopping floors, and wiping noses is not very exciting work. As more jobs become available for women, more of the "fairer sex" are combining a career at home with at least a part-time job in the labor market.

Why do women work? Bischof suggests a variety of reasons:[16] more free time (because of labor-saving devices in the home), a tendency for people to marry earlier (this leads to earlier childbearing and more free time in middle life), a need to help meet the high cost of living, a desire to get the "extras" which embellish our lives, a need to help put the college-age children and/or husbands through school, a desire to attain more status, a wish to return to the profession for which one was trained, and a desire to escape the boredom many women find at home.

Women who are homemakers need at times to be encouraged in their labors. They must realize that along with the joys and frustrations of being a housewife, they have the responsibility of molding young lives and maintaining a stable home. This is surely one of the most significant responsibilities that God gives. Sometimes organizations of young mothers can meet together in the church and, while one or two baby-sit, the others can experience a time of sharing and Bible study. Then for those who are more free to be away from the home, the church can provide opportunities for service in the church and community.

Normally women's groups run under their own leadership, and no church leader should downgrade their importance.

THE HANDICAPPED

A person's physical capabilities and intelligence have an important influence on his vocational choice and adjustment. For the individual with a severe physical disability or for the person with below-average mental ability, there is a drastic limitation in the number of available jobs. Even when he finds a position, the handicapped person has adjustment problems that the rest of us do not face. Fortunately most larger communities have counselors who are specially trained to help the handicapped with these problems, but this does not absolve the church of responsibility. The follower of Christ cannot ignore the lame, the blind or the otherwise disabled person. Because of the importance of understanding and counseling the handicapped, this topic is given more extensive treatment in a later volume of this series.

THE CHURCH LEADER'S ROLE

Vocational guidance counseling has now become a separate profession with its own techniques, journals, training, and specialists.* Since most church leaders have

*See especially the *Personnel and Guidance Journal* published by the American Personnel and Guidance Association, 1607 New Hampshire Avenue N.W., Washington, D. C. 20009.

no special expertise in this field, it is easy to conclude that the problems of vocational counseling should be left to someone better trained. Books on pastoral counseling often overlook this topic, failing to emphasize that the church leader can, in fact, make an important contribution to the vocational decisions of his congregation. Especially in rural areas or in places where there is inadequate occupational guidance in the schools, the church leader is sometimes the only available vocational counselor. Often the pastor or youth worker, though lacking the special skills and tools of the professional vocational counselor, nevertheless is especially respected by the job seeker and hence sought out as a counselor. Since he knows the family and since he—unlike most professionals—realizes the importance of God's will in vocational choice, the church leader is able to give special help.[17] In addition to more traditional vocational guidance, he can give spiritual counsel, provide information about church-related occupations, and write good letters of recommendation.

## SPIRITUAL GUIDANCE

When Jeremiah was called to be a prophet, he learned that there had been a divine plan for his life even before he was born (Jer. 1:5). The same was true of John the Baptist whose life work was described in detail prior to the time of his conception (Lk. 1:13-17). Whether or not God has a similar plan for every life today is a debatable issue, and the answer depends somewhat on one's theology. All Christians agree, however, that God expects His followers to yield their whole lives to Him (Ro. 12:1) and to serve Him faithfully (Ps. 2:11; Col. 3:23-24; Heb. 9:14). To do this we have been given different gifts, abilities and responsibilities (Ro. 12:3-8; 1 Cor. 12), and it is our duty to develop and use them in the best way possible.

How can one discover and be sure that he is making the best use of his divinely given gifts? How can one most effectively serve God? How do we discover a divine will for our lives? These are important questions which must concern believers of every age and must be considered whenever we seek employment, change jobs, or decide if we should remain where we are.

In counseling on these issues, it is important to recognize that the first step in finding God's will for us is to *want* it. Too often we decide what we want—vocationally and otherwise—and then go to God in prayer, seeking a divine stamp of approval. "I'll go where you want me to go, dear Lord," we sing, "but with the following stipulations...." This is not presenting ourselves wholly to Him; instead, it is trying to serve two masters—God's will and our selfish aspirations. Again, the first step in finding God's will is to *really want it*, but many people are never willing to make this decision.

Once we have completely committed ourselves and our careers to Christ, we must then *expect that He will lead.* The Scriptures assure us that God will guide in the decisions of life (Ps. 48:14; 73:24; Pr. 3:5-6; Jn. 16:13a), but often we ignore these promises. We assume instead that God is playing some kind of a hide-and-seek game, telling us that He expects us to serve, but making it next to impossible for us to discover where and how.

Finally, it is necessary to *recognize that God guides in a variety of ways.* Rarely today, if ever, does He speak to people as He did to Saul on the road to Damascus. Instead, He apparently directs through Scripture, through our intellectual abilities, and through the circumstances of life. In making a career choice, for example, if we have completely yielded ourselves to God and are expecting Him to lead, we can then move ahead confidently, using every available resource, including the broad guidelines of Scripture, psychological test results, occupational information, the recommendations of counselors, the availability or non-availability of jobs and educational opportunities, and our own personal evaluation of the situation.

Sometimes a counselee must be reminded that, unlike us, God isn't always in a hurry. He does not always reveal His will when we want it, nor does He always show us the whole divine plan at once. Abraham packed his possessions and moved his whole family in response to the divine command to move, even though he "went out, not knowing where he was to go" (Heb. 11:8, RSV). Many people today realize from personal experience that God still leads men in small steps.

## COUNSELING CONCERNING CHURCH VOCATIONS

Although all Christians are called to serve Christ, we are not all called to the same vocation. The body of Christ is composed of various occupational groups and nothing in Scripture suggests that professional missionaries, ordained ministers, seminary professors, or other "full-time Christian workers" are somehow more spiritual because of their church-related occupations. Surely God wants some people to be businessmen, secretaries, professional people, laborers, farmers, servicemen, union leaders, or housewives. These people are also members of the body of Christ (1 Co. 12). They serve where they are and have a witness in areas which might be inaccessible to the professional churchman. In the New Testament, when a man became a Christian, he committed his life to Christ, but there was no expectation that he would automatically leave his occupation and become a pastor or traveling missionary.

Having acknowledged this, we must also recognize that God does call some men and women to church-related occupations. As they contemplate careers, these people will want to discuss their ideas with a person who is in the field being considered. The pastor, Christian education director, chaplain, minister of music, missionary, evangelist, seminary professor, or other church worker can provide firsthand information about his work. When discussing his own vocation, for example, he can often rely on personal

126

experience to answer all of the questions listed in Table 4-1. Unlike many other professionals, the church worker can more easily demonstrate by example what he does and he can invite the counselee to "get the feel" of the ministry by participating in a limited fashion.

In counseling concerning church vocations it is important to remember that we cannot always be certain of God's will for someone else's life. We can describe the various opportunities available and help the counselee in his deliberations, but he is the one who, under God, must make the final decisions. Of course there is a real temptation to pressure someone to enter the ministry. Christian parents do this on occasion and so do pastors or Sunday school teachers. The need is so immense, the shortage of good personnel is so acute, the satisfaction of guiding someone into the ministry is so great, that it is easy to push a person into a field to which he is neither called nor attracted. [18]

## WRITING LETTERS OF RECOMMENDATION

The writing of good letters of recommendation is a laborious and time-consuming task, but it is a valuable way for the church leader to help others in their vocational planning. Many businesses and schools now send out forms in which the respondent can make his recommendation by checking from the several alternatives that are listed. This simplifies the task, but even the forms often leave a space for "further comments," and sometimes one might also want to include a letter with the form.

Instead of passing off these requests as a necessary nuisance, they should be taken seriously. In completing a form or writing a letter, remember that you have a responsibility to the applicant (it is best for him in the long run if we are honest—even if that prevents his application from being accepted), to the institution that seeks the information (as Christians we should not undermine their goal of getting capable people), to yourself and the name on the letterhead of your paper (it is of no credit to you if you "heartily recommend" someone who shouldn't be recommended) and to the Christ whom you follow.

The story is told of a man who once wrote a letter for someone whom he could not honestly recommend. "Dear Sir," the letter began, "if you knew the applicant like I know him your opinion of him would be the same as mine." Vaguely written letters get the writer out of a difficult and embarrassing situation, but they are of no value to anyone. More helpful are letters which state your qualifications for writing the letter, including how well and in what context you have known the applicant. They should be specific, give examples to support your opinions, be honest, and be as concise as possible. A conclusion stating whether or not you recommend the applicant is also helpful.

The following is an example, written to describe a hypothetical person:

DEAR SIR:

I am happy to write a letter in support of John Smith's application for admission to Trinity Evangelical Divinity School. I have known John for five years, during which time he and his family have been members of my congregation. I have visited in his home and he has been a periodic visitor to the parsonage. As president of the college class, he has consulted with me on several occasions during the past year.

During our contacts, John has always been tactful and willing to consider the suggestions of others. He is well liked by his peers (as evidenced by his election to the college class presidency) and willing to take responsibility. Before taking over as president, our college class was lagging, but John's enthusiasm and creative ideas (he led the class in starting a community coffee house, for example) have revived interest among the students. On those occasions when he has participated in our services, John has demonstrated good speaking ability. He is a keen student of the Scriptures and appears to be growing spiritually. The coffee house is one of several indications of John's desire to bring others to Christ.

Although he wants to enroll in seminary, John is still not certain about his vocational calling. His parents want him to enter the family business, and he has some inclination to enroll in a graduate school of business administration. This vocational uncertainty may affect his motivation to study at seminary, and there is a good possibility that he will not remain until graduation. Whatever his ultimate career, however, I believe that he could benefit from training at Trinity and that he would be a good person to have in your student body. For these reasons I am happy to recommend that he be accepted.

## SUMMARY

By being alert to the counseling techniques and the special problem areas discussed in this chapter, the church leader can do a great deal of effective vocational counseling. He serves in an important ministry when he guides people as they choose a life work, encourages those who are searching for a job, counsels with the vocationally frustrated and dissatisfied, directs people to occupational information or professional counselors, suggests opportunities for further schooling, helps counselees to find God's will for their lives, provides information about church vocations, and writes good letters of recommendation.

While much of this will be on a one-to-one basis, group vocational counseling in the church can also be very effective.[19] In youth meetings and adult discussion groups it can be helpful to many people if there is a discussion of such topics as the significance of work for the Christian, the importance of occupational planning, or the ways to find God's leading. Some churches have invited people from various occupations to give a short talk—one each week—

on the Christian in law, business, teaching, the ministry, etc.[20]

Many changes have transpired in the world of work since Adam and Eve were cast out of the garden and man was forced to labor by the sweat of his brow. Most of these changes have occurred within the past fifty years. With computers and today's technological revolution, even more cataclysmic shifts are bound to take place in the future. New occupations will appear and old ones will become obsolete. Labor-saving devices will doubtless become more prevalent, working hours will get shorter, and periods of leisure will get longer. Satisfaction that people now get from work will have to be found elsewhere.

Here is a real challenge for the church: to prepare people for a fluctuating world of work, to help them adjust to the changes, and to give them guidance as they seek to serve God in both their vocations and leisure-time activities.

# 5
## Special Counseling Situations

During the time when I was a graduate student living in a bachelor apartment, one of my friends surprised me with a little Christmas gift, a volume entitled *A Man's Cookbook*. It was given, I am sure, in hope of developing some culinary expertise in an embryo psychologist whose cooking skills were limited to canned soup, hot dogs, and TV dinners. A couple of years later when I got married, I discovered that my bride had a small library of cookbooks and knew how to use them well. By following the directions in the recipes, she was able to produce a great variety of gourmet delights, some of which had fancy foreign names which neither of us could even pronounce.

Most people who have been involved in counseling have wished at times that they had a good psychological cookbook. A president of the Midwestern Psychological Association even went so far one year as to title his presidential address "Wanted—a Good Cookbook."[1] It would be convenient if we could take a person with a certain problem, measure his symptoms in some way, mix in a little counseling, and have him "turn out perfectly" according to some previously devised plan. But a counseling cookbook is impossible, for no two counseling situations are ever exactly the same. This is what makes our task so difficult— and so challenging.

However, there *are* similarities in counseling problems.

In spite of individual uniquenesses, people who are dying show a great deal of similarity in their behavior, and so do those who are seriously ill, grieving, or disabled. We make no attempt here to produce a counselor's cookbook, but we describe typical characteristics in six special counseling situations. Then techniques that others have found to be helpful are discussed for each of these.

## Counseling the Mentally Ill

Very often people who are mentally ill don't differ much from the rest of us except for the fact that the problems of life have become so overwhelming that it is difficult for them to behave or think efficiently. Frequently there are discouragement, anxiety, confusion, a sense of failure, a loss of self-esteem, and feelings of frustration because one has succumbed to the pressures of life. Sometimes there is withdrawal into a secure little world of fantasy or inebriation while other people seemingly ignore the problems with gay abandon.*

### COUNSELING WITH THE DISTURBED INDIVIDUAL

The church leader faces four important challenges as he works with these emotionally disturbed people and their families. *First*, he can recognize the signs of emotional turmoil.** Even when the symptoms are obvious, family members are sometimes reluctant to face the reality of the situation and to encourage their relative to seek professional help. This is especially true if the family harbors the view that mental illness is a disgrace. Then the symptoms are explained away as a "temporary upset" or the result of "working too hard" and there is a clinging to the hope that, given time, the unusual behavior will disappear.

*Mental illness is discussed in detail in vol. 3 of this series: *Fractured Personalities*.

**The signs and symptoms of abnormality are also described in *Fractured Personalities*.

In many cases this does happen, but more often the problems get worse and treatment is simply delayed. While encouraging the church leader to be alert in looking for symptoms, we would also caution against too quickly seeing problems where none exist. The pastor who sees a psychotic in every pew will soon lose his effectiveness as a counselor. The goal is to be alert to the presence of the signs of abnormality but to be somewhat cautious in responding to them.

*Second*, the counselor can help the disturbed person get competent treatment. Sometimes the church leader himself can do an effective job of counseling, but at other times he will want to encourage referral to a mental health professional or treatment center. When this is done the principles of referral outlined in chapter 2 should be utilized.

In considering referral, try to determine where the counselee can get the best possible help. Sometimes a private psychiatrist or psychologist will give the most effective treatment, but at other times it may be better to consider the psychiatric ward in a general hospital, a local mental health center, a private psychiatric hospital, or a nearby state or provincial hospital. In making this decision, the financial means of the family, the seriousness of the problem, and the known effectiveness of the various referral sources should all be considered, along with the general *welfare* of the patient and his family.

If commitment to a psychiatric hospital seems advisable, it is best if the patient agrees to this voluntarily, supported by the encouragement of the family and pastor. But if the patient is severely disturbed and unwilling to get help, legal commitment may be necessary. Procedures for this vary from state to state, and even when the church leader is familiar—as he should be—with local commitment procedures, it is best in such situations to work in conjunction with a competent medical person.

Regardless of the treatment selected, the pastoral

counselor should be a source of support and comfort to both the patient and his family. Admission to a mental hospital, for example, is often accompanied by considerable anxiety, loneliness and fear. The counselor must help all involved to accept the reality of the situation, encouraging everyone to work together so the treatment will be successful. [2]

The *third* role of the church leader in working with the severely disturbed is to minister to the hospitalized. The patient who is confused, lonely or hurt can be helped immeasurably by visits from concerned friends, but often church leaders are reluctant to visit. Often they don't know what to expect when they call on a mental patient, or they are afraid of being unwelcome or are unsure of what to say. A good ground rule is to call on the mental patient as you would call on anybody else. Keep the visit brief; be cheerful and understanding; use prayer and the Scriptures (but keep this short and avoid scriptural passages which are likely to be misinterpreted by a patient whose thinking may be distorted); be encouraging, but avoid making promises that you cannot keep or taking sides if the patient is complaining or critical. Sometimes a patient will not want to talk, while at other times he may be extremely critical and antagonistic. This should not be taken personally, for it is probably part of his problem; the mere fact that you stay for a while and return for subsequent visits can, in the words of Maves, one hospital chaplain, "be one of the most constructive contributions to the patient's recovery." [3] The visits can be even more beneficial if you talk with the patient's doctor—before the first visit, if possible. This will help you understand the situation better and minister more effectively to the patient and his family, both during hospitalization and later.

Following hospitalization, the church leader has his *fourth* opportunity: helping the patient during the time of rehabilitation. Many pressures of family and community living which may have contributed to the "breakdown" in the first place, are still around when the patient leaves the hospital. In addition there is, for some, embarrassment over being an "ex-mental patient." Church leaders, as well as members of the congregation, must learn to accept the former patient and welcome him back into the church. This does not mean that we should pamper him, overwhelm him with a lot of people, treat him as an invalid, rigidly avoiding terms such as "crazy" or "mentally ill" or otherwise respond as if we fear an immediate relapse. The former patient should be welcomed back, encouraged, and treated as any other person who has been hospitalized.[4] Patients differ, however, so someone from the church should be in contact with the doctor, who can often give helpful suggestions to enable the church as a whole to facilitate the patient's readjustment to his community.

COUNSELING WITH THE FAMILY

When a relative develops mental illness, many families feel this is a major crisis. The patient's unusual behavior, the social stigma which still surrounds "mental illness," and the necessary readjustments when a relative is hospitalized, all put pressure on the family unit. Often there are confusion, anxiety and misunderstanding. For some families the crisis pulls everyone together, but for others the situation causes disintegration.

The church leader can help the disturbed patient's family in several ways, according to Clinebell.[5] First, he can help them recognize and accept the fact that the person is, indeed, emotionally disturbed. Then he can help the family and the patient get competent treatment. Since the family may be confused or uncertain about what is happening, the church leader can maintain a counseling relationship which informs, permits expression of feelings, encourages discussion of "why God would permit something like this," gives encouragement, and helps the family to increased dependence on God. Relatives can be helped to discuss and accept their feelings about mental illness in the family, encouraged to make hospital visits, and guided as they prepare to receive the patient back home when he is released from the hospital. Then the counselor can keep in contact with the whole family, including the patient. During the time of hospitalization and later, there may be times when the family will profit from more tangible help in the form of food or financial aid (Ja. 2:14-16).

OTHER CONSIDERATIONS

Since the church leader's own attitudes toward mental illness probably will be reflected in his counseling, it is important to develop some understanding of abnormal behavior before a need arises to counsel with disturbed persons and their families. Early discussion of one's attitudes and insecurities with a more experienced counselor can often be helpful.

Popular books and articles on mental illness often tend to be optimistic in discussing the effectiveness of professional treatment. This optimism is largely justified since most mental patients *are* released from treatment and many never do experience a relapse. But this should not hide the fact that some patients who enter a mental hospital stay there for life. These people may show no appreciation for the interest and visits of family or church members. Consequently, visitors eventually stop coming, and the patients are cast aside as "incurable inmates of the back wards," ignored by all except a few underpaid nurses and ward aides. Families should be encouraged to keep up their interest in the patient, but at the same time, family members must be helped to "pick up life" and carry on, realistically facing the fact that a hospitalization may be permanent.

COUNSELING THE PHYSICALLY ILL

When a person becomes physically ill much more is

involved than the malfunctioning of his body and the development of physical symptoms. Sickness brings, in addition, a number of psychological reactions such as anxiety, frustration and uncertainty both in the patient and his family. When an illness leads to financial strain, this can cause worry, and when the sickness disrupts routines in the home there must be readjustments in the family's customary way of life. This is especially so if the breadwinner or his wife is hospitalized or otherwise unable to carry on as usual.

Houts suggests that three characteristic periods occur in an illness: [6] The *transition period* from health to sickness may be sudden (as with a heart attack) or very gradual (as with cancer). Sometimes the person does not want to face his symptoms and avoids seeing a doctor in hopes that the physical problems will clear up spontaneously or in response to home remedies. When the symptoms persist or the sudden onset of serious illness makes denial impossible, it still takes time to adjust to the realization that "I am no longer healthy but am sick and may be this way for a long time."

In the *treatment period*, the person faces his symptoms and gives himself over to medical treatment, but this can also be a time of difficulty. In addition to the physical discomfort there is often fear of the unknown. "What is really wrong with me?" the patient wonders. "Will the doctors make an accurate diagnosis?" "Will I get better and, if so, how long will it take?" "Will we be able to pay for all of this?" "How will the family get along while I'm sick?" When hospitalization is required, the patient, who may be accustomed to independence, suddenly becomes dependent on others. For some, even such private activities as taking a bath or going to the toilet can be accomplished only with the help of a stranger. When it seems so important to be in a familiar setting, the patient finds himself in the midst of the unfamiliar—far removed from the tender care of his loved ones. If visitors call, he often is frustrated when he cannot be as well groomed as he would like. Then, of course, the family also must readjust and shift some responsibilities during the time of treatment.

In the *convalescence* period the person and his family slowly make the transition from sickness back to health. This can be a smooth process but it may also be fraught with difficulties. The patient may have discovered that he likes being dependent and free from his usual responsibilities. Family members may have learned to enjoy some of the new roles that they have taken on and may not want to revert to the way things were previously. Without the family being aware of what is happening, some of these attitudes in an unconscious way can lead to family conflict and a slowing down of the physical healing.

## COUNSELING THE PATIENT AND THE FAMILY

When He was on earth, Jesus spent a great deal of time ministering to the sick and, as His followers, we should be grateful for the privilege of doing likewise. The church leader can be an encouragement to both the patient and his family during their time of crisis, and a reminder that the great Physician is aware and concerned about the physical problems of His children. We can pray for and with the people involved, encourage the ventilation of fears and frustrations, guide in their thinking about why God permitted this situation to arise, point to relevant passages of Scripture, and help in making practical decisions, such as how to handle the extra financial burden, how to rearrange family routines, or how to evaluate medical options that the doctor may present. In visiting the sick, certain guidelines should be remembered. These are summarized in Table 5-1.

## COUNSELING WHEN A CHILD IS SICK

When a child becomes sick, the church leader is presented with a unique counseling situation. Like adults, children feel pain, fear the unknown, dislike the strangeness of the hospital, and do not want to be separated from loved ones. Unlike adults, young children do not worry about finances

# Table 5-1

# Guidelines for Visiting the Sick

### For All Patients

Visit frequently but keep the visits brief.

Let the patient take the lead in shaking hands.

Stand or sit where the patient can see you easily. The side of the bed is more suitable than the foot of the bed.

Give the patient freedom to talk freely, and listen carefully as he does so.

Use your resources as a Christian: prayer, Scripture, encouraging comments, etc. Whether you pray audibly should be determined by the Holy Spirit and the situation—the patient, his spiritual background, the people present, etc. Suggest prayer rather than ask if it is wanted, and keep it short.

Take appropriate precautions against contagious diseases.

Leave some devotional material.

Evaluate each visit to determine how they could be improved in the future.

### For Patients at Home

Telephone the home before the visit to make sure you call at a convenient time.

Try to call when there will be time for private discussion.

### For Hospital Patients

Upon arrival, check at the reception desk, introduce yourself and make sure that a visit at this time is acceptable.

Do not enter a room that has a closed door or a "no visitors" sign.

Try to call when there are not a lot of other visitors present.

### Dos and Don'ts

**Do:**

Be friendly and cheerful.

Be reassuring and comforting.

Help the patient relax.

Recognize that anxieties, discouragement, guilt, frustrations, and uncertainties may be present.

Give reassurance of Divine love and care.

Promise to pray for the patient during his illness—and act on your promise.

**Don't:**

Speak in an unnatural tone of voice.

Talk about your own past illnesses.

Force the patient to talk. Your silent presence can often be very meaningful.

Promise that God will heal them. Sometimes in His wisdom God permits illness to persist.

Visit when you are sick.

Talk loudly.

Sit, lean on, or jar the bed.

Visit during meals.

Whisper to family members or medical personnel within sight of the patient.

Share information about the diagnosis.

Question the patient about the details of the illness.

Tell the family how to decide when presented with medical options (but help them to decide).

Criticize the hospital, treatment or doctors.

Spread detailed information about the patient when you complete your visit.

or the seriousness of their illness, but they have a more limited understanding of what is happening, why they are suffering, or why people in white clothes stick them with needles or give bad-tasting medicines. For many children, hospitalization is interpreted as parental rejection or even punishment for past behavior. Often hospitalized children, especially those who are between two and four years old, protest at first, but when they discover that the protests are not getting them out of the hospital they slip into a period of despair and discouragement. Then they become increasingly apathetic, developing an "I don't care if my parents visit me" attitude.[7] After they get home such children may be demanding and overdependent since this is their way of asking for acceptance and reassurance.

The church leader has a ministry both to the child and to the family—especially the parents. How one counsels with a child will depend largely on the age and level of understanding, but children should always be reassured and not deceived. Familiar objects like teddy bears or blankets can give extra security, and sometimes the child appreciates a toy or gift of flowers from the other children at Sunday school. Since children are often unable to verbalize their fears and other feelings, the counselor should be especially alert to nonverbal clues. Often by one's attitude and bearing it is possible to create in the child a feeling of trust and a realization that "everything will be OK; they won't forget me." It is also possible to pray with the child and to assure him that "Jesus will be helping you while you're sick." By supportive counseling with the parents, we also can help the child indirectly because when he senses that his parents are calm, he feels greater assurance.

Often it is difficult for parents to feel this calmness, however, for as every parent knows, there is nothing more heartrending than to look into the face of a little sick child who doesn't understand. Such parents often appreciate support from a Christian friend who is willing to listen, encourage, and simply be present.[8] If the illness is serious, the parents may experience various emotions, some of which come and then go, only to return later. Denial, expectant hope, dazed disbelief, anxiety, anger (sometimes directed at the doctor, or the pastor, or God), guilt, frustration and grief, have all been seen in parents of seriously ill children.[9] It is helpful if these feelings can be verbalized and discussed, along with the question of "Why has it happened?" In addition, the comfort of prayer and the Scriptures should be an important part of a ministry of counseling with parents, and grandparents as well.

## Counseling the Dying

Death has always been surrounded by fear, anxiety and unhappiness. Even Christians, who believe that to be absent from the body is to be present with the Lord (2 Co. 5:8), shrink from thoughts of death and are uncomfortable in its presence.[10]

In an attempt to study how people react when faced with their own death, four theological students approached a psychiatrist several years ago at the University of Chicago Hospital. After meeting considerable resistance from hospital personnel who wanted the patients to be "left alone," the psychiatrist and her seminary students began interviewing terminally ill patients. Their findings, which have been published in a very interesting book, shed considerable light on the attitudes of the dying and how these people can be counseled.[11]

### UNDERSTANDING THE DYING

On the basis of carefully conducted psychiatric interviews with over one hundred terminally ill patients, Dr. Kübler-Ross has observed five stages that people go through as they approach death:

*First stage: Denial and isolation.* "No, it can't happen to

141

me" is the initial reaction of the patient when he learns or suspects that his sickness is terminal. This denial is a defense used by all patients, especially at the beginning of their illness. None of us wants to believe that our own death is imminent, and it helps people to handle the shock if they can periodically deny the truth of the diagnosis. Sometimes there is a vascillation between denial and acceptance which persists while the patient is slowly getting used to the idea.

*Second stage: Anger.* Patients can't keep denying the truth forever, and slowly they come to acknowledge the fact that they really are dying. Such a realization is accompanied by anger and resentment. "Why me?" they wonder. "Why couldn't it have been somebody who is old or alone or of no use to society?" Often this frustration and anger lead the patient to be critical of hospital personnel and highly demanding. Sometimes this even results in turning against loved ones, criticism of the pastor who visits, and anger against God. When this happens, the family members are often surprised and bewildered. They take the verbal attack personally, failing to realize that the patient's anger is really irrational—but normal—lashing out in response to a frustrating situation. At this time the patient needs understanding from loved ones, not an arguing back in hurt indignation.

*Third stage: Bargaining.* Little children who don't get their way by throwing a tantrum often resort next to a charming manner in which they try to persuade others to give them favors. The terminally ill person tends to act in a similar manner. Following the period of anger there is a time of bargaining for longer life or a freedom from pain. "God, give me a little longer," they may ask, "and I'll serve You faithfully for the rest of my life."

*Fourth stage: Depression.* As the illness lingers on, discouragement sets in. This is commonly of two types: Reactive depression, as the name implies, comes as a reaction against the illness and its effects. A patient may be discouraged, for example, because he misses his family, cannot enjoy his hobby, is unable to attend church, or is physically less attractive than before. The second type, preparatory depression, is really a form of grief as he anticipates the future. He may be a believer who looks forward to the "far better" time after death, but he is concerned about the loved ones who will remain and perhaps experience great difficulties when he is gone.

*Fifth stage: Acceptance.* Few patients keep resisting to the end; if the illness has been long, most eventually reach a stage of acceptance. This should not

> be mistaken for a happy stage. It is almost void of feelings.... This is also the time during which the family needs usually more help, understanding, and support than the patient himself. While the dying patient has found some peace and acceptance, his circle of interest diminishes. He wishes to be left alone or at least not stirred up by news and problems of the outside world....Our communications then become more nonverbal than verbal.[12]

Such patients may not want to talk, but they are comforted in knowing that they are not forgotten, even when the end is near.

*Hope.* There are broad individual differences in the way people approach death. The five stages may not be seen in everyone, especially if the length of illness is short. The approach to death may differ if one has a strong assurance that he will soon be with Christ. Regardless of one's religious convictions, however, it has been noticed that almost all terminally ill patients show at least some hope. The belief that "I might still get better" persisted throughout all stages and was so common in Dr. Kübler-Ross' patients that she concluded, "If a patient stops expressing hope, it is usually a sign of imminent death."[13]

## COUNSELING THE DYING

The place to begin in any ministry to the dying is with

our own attitudes. Most of us—including Christians—do not like to think about death. Perhaps many believers unconsciously expect that they will be among those who will avoid death and go directly to be with Christ (1 Th. 4:16-17). Whatever the reason, we frequently avoid discussing our own death and, in so doing, we leave a number of important decisions for the surviving spouse to make during the first hours of grief. Medical personnel, family members, and even pastors or other church leaders tend to avoid the dying patient, perhaps because we feel uncomfortable in his presence. Even when a chaplain or pastor calls, there is frequently a tendency to read a passage of Scripture and lead in prayer, but to avoid all reference to death or to the needs and concerns of the dying.[14] A careful consideration of the biblical statements about death, thinking about one's own death, and a discussion of funeral arrangements with one's family need not be an unhealthy dwelling on morbid events. Instead, it is an exercise which will make death easier when it comes and will enable us to more openly and comfortably discuss the subject when we counsel with the dying and their families.

Such counseling must be characterized by availability and genuine concern. The counselor must be flexible enough so that he can, when necessary, discuss fears and frustrations, bring comfort and encouragement from the Scriptures, or simply sit in silence. He can help the family to understand the reactions of the dying and he can recognize that relatives also go through stages similar to those of the patient. Sometimes he can help in the discussion of practical plans for the future, and he should encourage those involved to recognize and talk about the guilt that is so often present at the time of death.

Whether or not the patient and his family should be told that the illness is terminal is an issue that physicians and others still debate. One study has shown that 80 to 90 percent of physicians rarely tell their patients that a disease is terminal, but almost 80 percent of the patients say they want to be told. [15] Kübler-Ross suggests that most people know intuitively when they are dying, and for this reason it is usually best to face the reality of the situation openly. This frees both patient and family to discuss the future and to better communicate with each other. Once again, however, there can be no cookbook rules on this issue since each situation is different. It hardly seems wise to assure the patient of his recovery when such might not be the case, but neither is it good to emphasize coming death when the situation may not be that serious. Whenever possible, the pastoral counselor should be in contact with the patient's physician so that there can be cooperation in ministering to the needs of the dying patient and his family.

## COUNSELING THE GRIEVING

Even when death comes at the end of a long terminal illness, grief is a hard burden to bear. It involves a number of emotions, including sorrow, despair, anxiety, guilt, loneliness, anger, confusion, futility, and an overbearing sense of loss as someone who has long been part of us is now taken away for the rest of our lives.

Usually grief begins with a *period of shock*. When we learn that a loved one has died, there is often dazed disbelief, sometimes accompanied by physical symptoms such as nausea, faintness, stomach pains or throbbing headaches. Before the time of the funeral, the mourner has usually entered a *period of intense grief*. Copious weeping, intense yearning for the lost person, self-condemnation because of past times when we were inconsiderate, and preoccupation with memories of the deceased are all common in the weeks following the death. During this time there may be insomnia, loss of appetite, stomach upsets, restlessness, general irritability, and outbursts of anger. Sometimes there are periods of silent despair and a general sense of futility. [16]

In the Christian there are frequent prayer and searching of the Scriptures, interspersed with questions of "Why?" and sometimes with anger directed toward God. Later, perhaps after a month or two, the mourner slowly moves into a long *period of readjustment.* Life with its challenges must be picked up again but without the departed loved one being present. This includes a return to work, a resumption of normal activities, and some involvement in social affairs, but the sadness still remains. A lot of the enthusiasm is gone out of life, and frequently there are daydreams and memories of the departed one. Anniversaries and holidays may present the mourner with special reminders of his grief. "This is the first Christmas without Mother" or "John would have enjoyed being here for your birthday party" are poignant comments that express a lonely yearning.

## NEEDS OF THE GRIEVING

Sigmund Freud, who wrote about so many aspects of human behavior, also wrote about grief. He suggested that to accept the loss of a loved one and to resume a somewhat normal life again require pain and a lot of hard work. He called it the "work of mourning." To do this work successfully, certain needs must be met. W. F. Rogers, an experienced hospital chaplain, has listed the needs as follows: [17]

*The need for support from others.* At a time of grief it is important to have others, including people from the church, who can be present or available to listen, share and help.

*The need to accept the reality of the loss.* The intellectual knowledge that someone has died as well as the emotional acceptance of this fact are often two different issues. The mourner must go through the painful process of accepting the reality of the loss—a process which usually takes several months. To do this there is often a need to talk about the departed one, to relive past memories, and to remind oneself that the loss has actually occurred.

*The need to express sorrow.* When He arrived at the home

of Mary and Martha following the death of their brother, Jesus openly wept (Jn. 11:35). This may seem strange when we consider that Jesus knew in advance that Lazarus would be restored to life (Jn. 11:11-15), but by His example the Lord showed that the expression of sorrow is quite appropriate even among those who know that the departed one is "with Christ; which is far better" (Phil. 1:23). Therefore, the church leader must permit and encourage the outpouring of feelings, for this is a necessary part of grieving—for believers and nonbelievers alike.

This expression of sorrow takes two forms—weeping and talking. Before the bereaved can rebuild his life for the future, he must be allowed to talk about the days gone by and about the events immediately surrounding the death.[18] Well-meaning and perhaps embarrassed friends who tell the mourner to "cheer up" and "forget about it," or pious comforters who announce that "the real believer won't cry," are preventing the grieving person from meeting a very important need in his life.

*The need to verbalize hostility and guilt.* Books and articles on grief make frequent reference to the anger and hostility that are often experienced by grief-stricken persons.[19] Sometimes the anger is directed toward other people or toward God, and sometimes there is anger with the person who in dying has caused all of the present problems. Such anger may seem irrational, but it is a commonly observed reaction to frustration. Also common is anger directed inward toward oneself. This is really self-condemnation for what was said or not said, done or not done, while the dead person was alive. When the mourner thinks about his past life or when he realizes that he is angry with God or the deceased, there are often great feelings of guilt. Sometimes expensive funerals or large memorial gifts are really unconscious attempts by the grieving to atone for a guilty conscience. Such spending is not necessarily bad, providing it does not deplete the family resources.

147

*The need to establish new relationships.* The grieving person must find others who can provide the security and satisfaction that the former relationship provided. This is a difficult and time-consuming process which can be accompanied by guilt if the mourner feels that in building new friendship he is also being unfaithful to the deceased. With the loss of a spouse the problem is accentuated, since ours is a society where people do things in couples and often there is little place for the unattached. All these needs present the church leader with a real challenge as he works with the grieving over a period of months.

## UNHEALTHY REACTIONS TO GRIEF

Since there are large individual differences in the way people respond to grief, it is impossible to say what is "normal." Sometimes, however, the grieving person shows behavior which is so unusual that it indicates an unhealthy reaction. Excessive self-condemnation, stoic denial of grief, getting involved in a host of busy activities, taking on a number of physical symptoms, excessive drinking, antisocial behavior, suicide attempts, intense anger, and complete withdrawal from social activities can all indicate unhealthy responses to grief, especially if they are present several months after the funeral. Sometimes professional counseling is necessary for such people, but often the church leader and others can be very helpful as they guide the mourner to a more realistic resolution of his grief.

## COUNSELING THE GRIEVING

The pastor and members of the congregation play at least three major roles in counseling with the sorrowing. First, they *bring the comfort of the Scriptures.* The Bible pictures death as a great gain for the believer and something to be welcomed (Phil. 1:21). By His own death and resurrection Christ overpowered death so that the believer is assured of everlasting life in the presence of the risen Lord (Jn. 3:16; 14:1-3; 1 Co. 15:54-57; 1 Th. 4:13-18). For those who mourn,

Jesus promised comfort (Mt. 5:4), and He described the Holy Spirit as "the Comforter" (Jn. 14:26) who would be present in times of grief. Over the centuries great numbers of believers have felt this "peace of God, which passeth all understanding" (Phil. 4:7), but this can never be described or analyzed by the writer of a psychology book. Such a divine comfort is supplemented by the comfort that believers show for one another in times of sorrow. Of course, even nonbelievers turn to religion—if not the Scriptures—in times of grief. As Gorer has observed, many people in our society are born, raised and married without religion, but at the time of death there is a widespread turning to God and the comforts of religious doctrine and practice.[20] But while man-centered religion can bring comfort, there can be little cause for hope among nonbelievers (1 Th. 4:13). Only Christ gives real peace, and we should remind one another of this in times of sorrow (1 Th. 4:18).

Closely related to this is the role of the church leader at the time of the funeral. Several years ago a powerfully written book attacking the "funeral industry" skyrocketed to popularity in the United States, stimulated great debate about the tactics of funeral directors, and brought forth defensive counterattacks from numerous morticians.[21] While Jessica Mitford's book was undoubtedly a biased distortion which overemphasized the unscrupulous practices of a small minority, the resulting discussion did much to clarify the real values of a funeral.

The funeral is a ceremony for the living—not for the dead. In the first place, it forces people to face the painful truth that death has, in fact, occurred. A memorial service without the body being present may be much easier to bear, but it does little to bring home the harsh reality that must be faced eventually. In addition, the funeral is an opportunity for friends to express their concern and support for the bereaved. For Christians, the funeral is also an opportunity to worship and to give witness of the hope that is within.

A Christian funeral is not...an occasion to say a few pretty words or listen to sentimental music. The purpose is Christian worship. The goal is to focus attention on the greatness and goodness and everlasting nature of God. Congregation and mourners alike should be caught up in a worship experience that transcends circumstances, that strengthens and undergirds. [22]

In ministering to the grieving, the church leader can *help in the planning for a funeral.* (Ideally, of course, Christians should think about this before they die.) He can help the family to make decisions about the type and cost of the coffin, the place of the funeral (church or funeral home), and the details of the service. He can lead in a worship experience which "strengthens and undergirds," which expresses the comfort of Christ and the concern of friends, but which also helps the mourner to accept the reality of death.

The third role of the church leader is to *guide during the period of readjustment.* When the funeral is over, the flowers have wilted, and the relatives have gone home, the months which follow are often very lonely and painful. It is here that the concerned Christian tries to be available to bring the comfort of friends and the Scriptures, and to guide as the mourner works to satisfy the needs outlined in the preceding pages.

## DEATH AND THE YOUNG CHILD

After completing a study of almost 1,000 bereaved people, Gorer, an English writer, concluded that the death of a child is "the most distressing and long-lasting of all griefs.... In such a case it seems to be literally true, and not a figure of speech, that the parents never get over it." [23] That life should end for a little child with so much potential is a terrifically painful realization, even if we expect to see him again in eternity (2 Sa. 12:23).

It can also be difficult to explain to a child that someone whom he loves has died. The way in which this is presented and the words that are used depend largely on the child's age and level of understanding. It should be recognized that young children under five do not understand the finality of death, nor do they know how this will affect them. Older children, especially those who are nine or ten years of age and older, have a clearer understanding of death and a more adultlike ability to experience grief. For children of all ages it is important to openly discuss the death and to give reassurance that the surviving child is loved and will be cared for, no matter what the circumstances.[24]

## COUNSELING THE PHYSICALLY DISABLED

During His earthly ministry, Jesus showed a deep concern for the physically disabled. He ministered to the blind, the deaf, the lame, and others who were physically infirm, and many of His followers did likewise, but today the situation seems to have changed. While it may be true that some churches provide a "haven" for the disabled,[25] it is probably more accurate to conclude that today most Christians ignore, or at least make little effort to reach, those who are handicapped because of physical disabilities.

A physically disabled person is one whose body has a defect or impairment which partially hinders or interferes with the person's ability to function normally in the society. The person with paralyzed legs, for example, has a part of his body that is not functioning. Because of this, he cannot walk normally and must remain confined to a wheelchair. Notice, however, that he is only partially handicapped. He can still think, use his arms, see, hear and talk. This illustrates an important truth about the disabled person. While there are things which he *cannot* do, there are also things which he *can* do.[26] This is important to remember in counseling.

People who are disabled from birth apparently adjust smoothly to their condition. In the 1960s when several thousand babies were born in Germany without arms or legs, the government established clinics to provide artificial limbs and to help the children adjust. It was discovered, however, that the children were quite happy without the prostheses and seemingly were little motivated to adjust to them.[27] It is always frustrating to overcome a physical disability, but those who are born with a defect cope with it from birth, do not know what it feels like to have the body functioning normally, and thus don't miss what they have never known.[28]

Undoubtedly the situation is more difficult when a person is disabled later in life. Fink has identified four stages that such people go through: *shock* when the disability first occurs; *retreat* behind a number of psychological defenses which enable one to temporarily avoid facing the full impact of the situation; *acknowledgment* in which the person slowly faces the almost overwhelming implications of the disability; and *adaptation* in which the person adjusts to his disabled condition.[29] A somewhat similar set of reactions has been suggested by Proelss, a chaplain who identified what he called "three D-A clusters."[30] The first of these—depression and anger—involves deep discouragement accompanied by hostility and resentment. The disabled person is sad and frustrated because of the events that have entered his life. Stage two—denial and acceptance—represents a period of struggle and vascillation. At times there is a refusal to admit that the handicap exists or will persist, but slowly the truth is accepted. The third stage—dependence versus autonomy—represents a learning to live as best as one can within the limits imposed by the handicap. The disabled person often wants to be as independent as possible, but he realizes that some dependence on others is inevitable. To accept this need for dependency, to not attempt more than one can, but also to **avoid** a passive overdependence, is a difficult balance to attain.

The physically disabled person must make a number of psychological adjustments that those with a more "normal" physique can avoid. For example, he must adjust to being different. Little children look at him with open curiosity while adults glance at him in a more subtle way, avoid him, or sometimes treat him with scorn. Like everyone else, the disabled person wants to be treated with respect and to feel that he is a worthy individual, but this is a difficult goal to reach. Because of his physical limitations, a number of occupations and activities are closed to him. Even if he does get a job, the disabled worker can never be sure that he will be accepted, or that he will be able to manage the stairs or other situations that the nondisabled handle with ease. While the handicapped have normal sexual desires, they have few opportunities for dates and a lower-than-average likelihood of getting married. The author remembers vividly a mildly disabled young lady of thirty-one who approached him after a church service one night. "You're a psychologist," she said with tears in her eyes. "Tell me why I've never had a date. I want to get married like anyone else."

## COUNSELING THE DISABLED

The first task in counseling the physically disabled is to convey acceptance. We must treat the counselee as a person of worth who has characteristics that are desirable, feelings that need to be expressed, needs that must be met, frustrations that must be overcome. This respect and accept-ance will not seem very genuine if limited to a handshake on Sunday morning or a periodic pep talk. If he wants to *appear* accepting, the counselor must really *be* accepting. If he cannot be accepting, he needs to take an honest look at his own attitudes and perhaps discuss them with some confidant.

As we accept the handicapped person, we must seek to

help him accept himself, to realistically evaluate his limitations, to overcome obstacles when he can, and to function as efficiently as possible with his limitations. He must come to recognize that, regardless of his handicap, he is an individual whom God loves and whom Christ came to redeem. We must guide in his spiritual growth, helping him to find and follow God's will for his life. Also, we must be willing to discuss questions of "Why?" and help him accept the difficulties in his life.

Handicapped teenagers and young adults have a special need for a counselor, be he a trained and sensitive minister, social worker, or other trained person. A pastor frequently is the one to whom the handicapped individual turns, for often his problems are in some way, if not directly, connected with his faith and outlook on life.

But having said this, it must be added that this type of pastoral counseling demands knowledge of the ramifications of the handicap itself, psychological understanding, counseling skills, and a deep and mature Christian faith. The pastor who is to be truly helpful needs to have an understanding of the limitations which the disability imposes. Perhaps the answers to these questions can be secured from the individual himself, or perhaps the pastor, with the individual's permission, should discuss the matter with a doctor, or social worker at the rehabilitation center where the individual is being treated.

This information will not only assist the pastor in coming to a better understanding of the handicapped person or persons in his congregation, but will help him determine how realistic or unrealistic these persons may be.[31]

The church leader is not the only person involved in working with the handicapped. Parents (who often need understanding and encouragement themselves as they cope with their feelings and the special demands of their handicapped children), physicians, teachers, vocational counselors and others must work together to help the disabled. Members of the congregation must be encouraged to take an interest in the handicapped, to accept them as people, to help them get to the churches (which more often than not have stairs but no ramps for wheelchairs) and to guide in their spiritual, emotional, social and vocational development.

## COUNSELING THE DISADVANTAGED

Tom Skinner, the Harlem gang leader who turned to Christ and became an evangelist, has written of the evangelical flight to the suburbs when a neighborhood begins to change from white to black. Skinner notes that conservative churches move, sell their property to liberals, and leave a needed area without any sound evangelical witness.[32] We give freely to support missionaries in black Africa, orphanages in Asia, poor churches in Latin America, and even rescue missions on skid row, but we don't get too involved in meeting the needs of minority and disadvantaged groups, the uneducated, those who live in culturally impoverished rural areas, migrant and unskilled workers, skid-row dwellers and others. Some have suggested that we should also include many dwellers in high-rise apartments who are economically well off, but spiritually impoverished.

Regardless of whom we classify as disadvantaged, it should be recognized from the start that counseling with and ministering to people of other ethnic and socioeconomic groups is very difficult. I once had a long discussion with a white psychiatrist who works primarily with blacks in the inner city of Philadelphia. "If you are going to help these people," he stated, "you have to live among them and really get to know them." For years we have recognized this as a basic part of foreign missionary strategy, but at home we think we can drive into an impoverished area, counsel or witness effectively, and then retreat to our nice suburban residences.

In a book about the psychological stresses of the ghetto, psychiatrists Grier and Cobb suggest that blacks must regard every white man as a potential enemy unless proven otherwise.[33]  To counsel with any disadvantaged group we must expect to be rejected at first and treated as a potential enemy. We must have patience, Christian love, understanding, acceptance, and complete freedom from any holier-than-thou attitudes. All of this takes considerable time. It means that no man can minister effectively to all disadvantaged groups, and that few can spare the time to minister effectively with one. In spite of the difficulties, however, we cannot fulfill the Great Commission while ignoring the disadvantaged nearby. Every church leader should consider how his congregation, if not he himself, can have some impact on this difficult mission field which literally may be around the corner.

## THE QUESTION OF "WHY?"

Throughout this chapter and earlier in this book we have mentioned that people whom a church leader counsels ask "Why?" frequently. Why do I have this problem? Why did God let this happen? Why didn't it happen to someone else? Why do ministers say that God is loving and good when He permits such sadness and misery? These are difficult questions which should be pondered before they have to be answered in a counseling session. They are also theological questions which are out of the domain of psychology.

In the Bible the answers to "why" questions are not always clear. We do know that when God permits or brings about some stressful situation, He does so for a good purpose (Ro. 8:28). It may be to produce patience (Ja. 1:3), humility (2 Co. 12:7-10), or a deeper dependence on God (2 Co. 1:8-9). Sometimes it is an expression of divine love for us and, even though we may feel miserable at the time, the Scriptures describe those whom the Lord chastens as "blessed" (Ps. 94:12; Pr. 3:11-12; Rev. 3:19).

156

In counseling, the Christian leader can point the *counselee* to those passages of Scripture which deal with suffering (see especially 1 Peter and Job). He can guide as the counselee ventilates his feelings and seeks to find answers in the Scriptures. But he can also point to the example of Job. Though he suffered through a series of setbacks that would have overwhelmed most of us, and though his counselors only added to the problems, Job was never told why it all happened. God has a purpose (Job 1-2), but Job never knew what this was. In many cases the same is true today. So long as we live on earth, the ways of God are often beyond our comprehension (Ro. 11:33). We can ask why and try to find an answer—there is nothing wrong with that—but we must realize that God in His wisdom may not answer but instead require us to suffer in ignorance.

## SUMMARY

Counseling is difficult work requiring time, patience, understanding, skill, and a great deal of wisdom. Books on psychology can help us to anticipate and improve our skills, but in the privacy of a counseling session, the counselor can feel pretty lonely and anxious as he seeks to help another. We have summarized some counseling techniques and discussed some of the problems that might be faced by the church leader in his counseling work, but there has been no attempt to provide a cookbook—a series of dos and don'ts that would apply to every forseeable situation. This would be impossible! We have, instead, tried to provide an introduction to some common problem areas and to suggest some broad outlines for approaching these issues.

In working with the mentally ill and their families, the church leader can spot potential problems, encourage those involved to get treatment, minister during the time of hospitalization, and help the patient to readjust on his return to the community. Even in modern societies the emotionally disturbed are still widely looked upon with curiosity and suspicion. These attitudes must be countered when they appear in the family, in the congregation, or in the church leader himself.

Physical illness brings pain, uncertainty, and the disruption of family routines. At such a time, the church stands by to encourage, to guide in the expression of feelings, to provide tangible help, and to remind of the presence and concern of God. When the illness is terminal, the patient and family need help in accepting the prognosis and in preparing realistically for the future.

Following the death of a loved one, the long slow process of grieving presents the counselor with another challenge as he guides the bereaved through the days of shock, the funeral, and on during the many months of readjustment. The church leader brings support and comfort from the Scriptures, helping the bereaved to accept the reality of the loss, to express their feelings, and to slowly establish new relationships.

The physically disabled are restricted in the opportunities open to them. They must adjust to being different, to being at least partly dependent on others, and to being restricted in the available educational, vocational and marital choices. Too often these people are ignored by the church, but they need to experience the guidance of concerned Christians, and the knowledge of God's love for all men—regardless of physique.

In all of these situations and in many others, the counselee wants to know why he must suffer. The Scriptures give some answers to this question but often there can only be acknowledgment that God is sovereign and does not always share with finite minds the reasons for His infinitely wise decisions.

# 6
*Mental Health and Prevention of Abnormality*

Every year hundreds of people lose their lives in drowning accidents. Suppose the city council of a lakeside community is so concerned about this problem that they appoint a director of water safety. Charged with the responsibility of reducing water accidents, the new director hires and trains a crew of highly skilled lifeguards. A rescue station is built on the beach and a small fleet of boats is acquired. All of these preparations will be important when it comes time to rescue persons drowning in the lake. But the work of rescuing and saving the perishing is only part of a good water-safety program. It is just as important to teach people how to swim and to stay afloat when the waves are high or the currents are strong.

The need for rescue operations is increasing as the population expands, the pace of life becomes faster, pressures in the society become greater, and people become more willing to admit that they have emotional problems. There is a rising need for psychologists, psychiatrists, social workers, nurses, school counselors, pastoral counselors, and volunteer workers. Many mental-health clinics are understaffed and overburdened by long waiting lists. There is a great need for more highly skilled counselors and for rescue stations in the form of clinics, counseling centers, and psychiatric services in general hospitals. Within recent years there have been great increases in manpower and

and facilities, but research has shown that we can never catch up to meet our needs.[1] There can never be enough mental-health lifeguards to help all of the people who are mentally in deep waters. If we are to deal effectively with this situation, therefore, our only alternative is to teach people how to swim, that is, how to deal with the pressures of life. The creation of good mental health and the prevention of abnormal behavior are issues which must be of concern to church leaders as well as to professional counselors.

## MENTAL HEALTH

There are a number of words and phrases in the English language which are widely used, but which most people can only define vaguely, for example, "American way of life," "normal," "intelligence," "artistic," "happiness" and "success." Another example is "mental health."

Probably every psychologist would agree that mental health refers to something positive. More than the absence of "mental illness," it has been defined instead as "the ability to function effectively and happily as a person in one's expected role in a "group";[2] as "happiness experienced at a deep level";[3] and as "a state of being in which the person finds a satisfactory measure of fulfillment."[4] The Menninger Foundation of Topeka, Kansas, has substituted "emotional maturity" for "mental health" and listed the characteristics of maturity which are shown in Table 6-1.

Some psychologists have suggested that the terms "mental health" and "mental illness" should be eliminated altogether. When a person is ill, it is argued, something that is organically wrong causes symptoms in the body of a helpless victim. To be restored to health, the sick person must be treated exclusively by a physician who uses medical procedures. The patient has little responsibility in bringing about the cure, but instead is a passive recipient of the doctor's treatment. While some behavior abnormalities fit the above

160

## Table 6-1

## The Criteria of Emotional Maturity*

Having the ability to deal constructively with reality

Having the capacity to adapt to change

Having a relative freedom from symptoms that are produced by tensions and anxieties

Having the capacity to find more satisfaction in giving than receiving

Having the capacity to relate to other people in a consistent manner with mutual satisfaction and helpfulness

Having the capacity to sublimate, to direct one's instinctive hostile energy into creative and constructive outlets

Having the capacity to love.

*Copyright 1965, The Menninger Foundation. Reprinted by permission.

description, many do not. The brain-damaged person has a real illness, but what about the neurotic who has nothing organically wrong? Unlike a virus, the neurosis does not attack a helpless victim but may occur because of the neurotic's own irresponsible or unwise behavior. Often he can be helped by nonmedical counselors who, using counseling and other nonmedical procedures, expect the neurotic to take responsibility for the major part of his rehabilitation. Therefore, much of what we call "mental illness" is not illness at all. According to psychiatrist Thomas Szasz, "the notion of mental illness has outlived whatever usefulness it might have had and...now functions merely as a convenient myth" which helps people avoid facing the fact that they have some responsibility for the presence and elimination of the abnormal behavior in their own lives.[5] Regretfully, those who suggest that we eliminate the terms "mental illness" and "mental health" have failed to suggest more clearly defined alternatives. For this reason we will continue to use these more common terms, while at the same time recognizing their weaknesses.

Mental health is too large a concept to be defined in a few words. Instead, it is more realistic to see what mental health is *not* and then to list some of the characteristics that indicate good mental health. According to a group of professional counselors, mental health is *not*

1. Adjustment under all circumstances. There are many circumstances to which man should not adjust, otherwise there would be no progress.

2. Freedom from anxiety and tensions. Anxiety and tension are often prerequisites and accompaniments of creativity and self-preservation....

3. Freedom from dissatisfaction....

4. Conformity. One criterion of maturity is the ability to stand apart from the crowd when conditions indicate....

5. Constant happiness. In this imperfect world, a sensitive, mature person often experiences unhappiness.

6. A lessening of accomplishment and creativity. Mental health is characterized by the ability of the individual to use his powers ever more fully.
7. The absence of personal idiosyncrasies. Many such idiosyncrasies which do not interfere with function enrich the life of the individual and those who come in contact with him.
8. The undermining of authority. Mental health is characterized by the increased ability of the individual to use and respect realistic authority while deprecating the use of authority as an oppressive force....
9. Opposition to religious values. Mental health facilitates and complements the aims of religion inasmuch as it fosters the highest spiritual and social values. [6]

There is no sharp line between mental health and mental illness, between being normal and abnormal. Most people are someplace in between (see Fig. 6-1), and in all probability vascillate back and forth on the scale as problems and crises come into their lives.

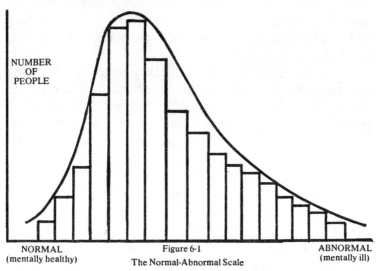

NUMBER OF PEOPLE

| NORMAL | Figure 6-1 | ABNORMAL |
| (mentally healthy) | The Normal-Abnormal Scale | (mentally ill) |

Almost nobody is completely normal (mentally healthy) or abnormal. Most of us are probably somewhere in between, although more people are toward the normal end of the scale.

163

## SOME CHARACTERISTICS OF GOOD MENTAL HEALTH

The mentally healthy person probably will show many of these more important characteristics of mental health:

*Social and emotional competence.* Mentally healthy persons generally behave in ways which are acceptable to the majority of people in the society. Each acts in accordance with the social roles typical for one of his age, sex, education, marital status and occupation. He respects the rights and needs of others, accepts responsibility for his own actions, tries to understand and appreciate the motives of others, and helps those in need. He is not immobilized by fear, anger, love or anxiety, but neither does he hide these and other emotions, pretending they do not exist.

*Satisfying interpersonal relations.* According to Erich Fromm, the famous psychoanalyst, man wants to be unique, but he also needs to be related to other people in bonds of mutual care, responsibility, respect and understanding.[7] The normal person has both superficial social contacts and intimate, deeply involved relationships with one or a few confidants. He avoids the extremes of social isolation and hectic overparticipation in social activities.[8] Occasionally he has the courage to let down his social mask and let others know him as he really is.[9]

*Self-examination and insight.* Many years ago Socrates said that "the unexamined life is not worth living." Jesus apparently had something similar in mind when He instructed His followers to look at the faults in their own lives before criticizing others (Mt. 7:1-5). When He instituted the Lord's Supper, Jesus told each man to "examine himself" before partaking of the elements (1 Co. 11:27-30).

If we honestly look at ourselves we should get some insight into our behavior and some appreciation for both our strengths and weaknesses. Of course, it is difficult to be objective in our self-examination and we should realize that no one ever achieves complete self-insight. But we will get along better if we have at least some self-understanding. It also helps if we have a sense of humor. Life is serious, but nevertheless the normal individual is able to get things in perspective and occasionally to laugh at himself and his circumstances.

*Self-acceptance and self-confidence.* Self-examination often reveals things about ourselves that we don't want to see, and can lead to pessimism, self-pity, self-rejection, and a loss of self-confidence. But the mentally healthy individual is not overwhelmed by his own weaknesses. Like many persons in Alcoholics Anonymous, he can pray, "God grant me the serenity to accept the things I cannot change, the courage to change the things I can, and the wisdom to know the difference." Recognizing his strong points along with the weak, he accepts himself for what he is, improves where he can, sets realistic aspirations, and works to build his self-confidence.

*Realistic approach to problems.* It is not healthy to evade problems, hide from them, or try to solve them through excessive worry, complaining, or procrastination.[10] Even though it may be painful, the healthy person faces his problems realistically and tries to arrive at successful solutions. To some extent this involves being organized, so that the individual is not overwhelmed by his problems and responsibilities but can handle them one at a time.

*Freedom from internal conflict, intense feelings of insecurity, and paralyzing anxiety.* The mentally healthy person cannot be immobilized by such internal tension and turmoil.

*Satisfying philosophy of life.* To be mentally healthy is to have some meaning to life and some purpose for living. The healthy person also holds values and moral principles which guide his behavior and influence his thinking.

The Bible contains many guidelines for a satisfying life. In Philippians 2, for example, we are admonished to think like Christ (v. 5) who was obedient and humble (v. 8). We are to do things without grumbling (v. 14) and to shine as examples of godly behavior "in the midst of a crooked and perverse generation" (v. 15, margin). But the really satisfying life comes only when we "confess that Jesus Christ is Lord" (v. 11) and invite Him to control our lives so that He will help us "want to obey Him, and...do what He wants" (v.13, Living Letters). This is old theology—some would call it old-fashioned—but it is good theology, and a basic requirement for real mental health.

*Love.* Once again, Fromm speaks clearly on this topic:

> There is hardly any word which is more ambiguous and confusing than the word "love." It is used to denote almost every feeling short of hate and disgust. It comprises everything from the love for ice cream to the love for a symphony, from mild sympathy to the most intense feeling of closeness. People feel they love if they have "fallen for" somebody. They call their dependence love, and their possessiveness too. They believe, in fact, that nothing is easier than to love, that the difficulty lies only in finding the right object, and that their failure to find happiness in love is due to their bad luck in not finding the right partner. But contrary to all this confused and wishful thinking, love is a very specific feeling; and while every human being has a capacity for love, its realization is one of the most difficult achievements. [11]

The love about which Fromm writes is an activity in which one respects and cares for another. There is a feeling of responsibility for the welfare of the loved person, as well as a desire to know and understand him. [12]

A more specific description of love is given in 1 Corinthians 13:

> Love is patient and kind; love is not jealous or boastful; it is not arrogant or rude. Love does not insist on its own way; it is not irritable or resentful; it does not rejoice at wrong, but rejoices in the right. Love bears all things, believes all things, hopes all things, endures all things. Love never ends (vv. 4-8, RSV).

166

We must make this love our aim (1 Co. 14:1), loving others as Christ loved us (Jn. 15:12). Such love comes with the help of God (1 Th. 3:12) and when we commit ourselves to the control of God's Holy Spirit (Gal. 5:16, 22). This is mentally healthy.

Complete normality is a rare state possessed only by people who are at peace with society, with themselves, and with God. The characteristics listed above are consistent with this threefold definition of mental health.

## PREVENTION OF ABNORMAL BEHAVIOR

There are two ways to prevent people from drowning: teach them how to swim and handle themselves in the water, so that they never get into trouble, or pull them out if they start to go under. Similarly, there are two common approaches to the prevention of abnormal behavior. We can work to prevent the development of new disorders (primary prevention), or we can try to spot mild disorders and prevent them from becoming more serious or prolonged (secondary prevention).

### PRIMARY PREVENTION

If we hope to prevent abnormal behavior from developing, we must reduce or eliminate early experiences that could be psychologically harmful, and we must teach people how to handle stresses of life. In preventing abnormality it is important to be alert to the biological, psychological, social and spiritual spheres of life.

*Biological prevention.* Good physical health and good mental health do not always go together, but they do frequently. If a person takes care of his physical needs, has a balanced diet, takes time for exercise and relaxation, avoids overindulgence in food, drugs or alcohol, and gets sufficient sleep, he will be better able to handle life's stresses. Also important are good maternal care during pregnancy, the immunization of children, and getting proper medical treatment when not feeling well. Geneticists are currently studying hereditary influences on behavior so that programs may be developed to "ensure that babies are born with better genetic endowment, or that couples who are likely to give birth to babies with inherited brain defects are advised against conception." [13]

*Psychological prevention.* Education is of crucial importance in preventing psychological disorders. Parents must learn how to live in harmony with each other and how to provide a home where there is a minimum of tension, neglect of children, overpermissiveness or overprotection. Children must be taught discipline and responsibility, must acquire the roles and social expectations of their society, must learn how to handle the stresses of life, and must be guided as they prepare for the future. In times of crises and other difficulties, there should be supportive friends or opportunities for counseling in the community. All of the characteristics of good mental health, discussed earlier in this chapter, are learned—usually during childhood. The home, school and church carry most of the responsibility for this learning.

*Sociological prevention.* Government and community programs geared to changing economic and social conditions can eliminate some situations that breed behavior deviation. By reducing unemployment, improving housing, providing better educational opportunities, and giving better medical care, the standard of living rises and some sociological predisposing and precipitating influences are eliminated. The government can do much in this area, but whether everything should be left to the government is a debatable issue which depends on one's politics. In spite of limited budgets, however, many community organizations—such as service clubs, PTA, united fund agencies, or concerned citizens' groups—are very successful in their efforts to improve community conditions.

It is also important that the government and community

give support to research efforts, for the more we know about the conditions which give rise to abnormal behavior, the better will be our preventive efforts. But we can only learn of these conditions through skilled efforts of psychologists, sociologists, psychiatrists, biologists, and others engaged in social research.

*Spiritual prevention.* By developing clear-cut moral standards, finding an enduring faith, and formulating a unifying philosophy of life, people are immunizing themselves against psychological collapse. Primarily the home and the church are responsible for instilling these moral standards, but many parents have ignored their duty, concluding that children should "decide what they believe when they get older." Likewise, many churches have cast aside biblical values, substituting a relativistic situational ethic which gives little guidance for confused young people. Equally undesirable is a church attitude which pretends ethical questions and problems do not exist and encourages young people to "keep on praying so that everything will be OK." Parents and church leaders must give guidance and encouragement as people face and seek solutions to life's difficult moral issues.

## SECONDARY PREVENTION

Once an emotional disorder has begun, three things can be done to "nip it in the bud" before it blossoms into a more serious abnormality.

*First, we must detect developing problems.* This is the responsibility of people in the community: teachers, doctors, employers, pastors, Sunday school teachers, etc. Of all these people, the church leader probably is in the best position for locating people with developing problems. He sees members of the congregation from week to week, knows their families, and can observe them in a variety of settings, including the church, home, and social gatherings.

Certainly nobody wants to be a psychological Sherlock

Holmes, trying to uncover and expose mental illness, [14] but often our common sense tells us that something is wrong. The overly aggressive child in the Sunday school, for example, the groggy adolescent in the high school, or the socially isolated college girl may be potential psychiatric casualties. It is a good idea to watch for high-risk groups such as children from broken homes, the grief-stricken, adolescents, the elderly, the physically ill, and the socially deprived, for all these have a higher than average likelihood of developing disorders. [15] Of course the careful observation of people must be done subtly and with complete concern for their welfare and right to privacy. If we suspect that something is wrong, it is well to watch for at least some additional information before moving to the second step in secondary prevention.

*The second step is getting the person to a place where he can be helped.* People with developing problems are often not very motivated to get help. Their "problem" may not be bothering them much (in cases such as drinking, drug use, sex deviations or some neurotic reactions, they may actually be enjoying their abnormal behavior), so there is little desire to take the time or effort to engage in counseling. Motivation is often improved when the person is helped to see the logical outcome of his present behavior, encouraged to believe there is nothing wrong with getting help (attitudes about "head shrinkers" and their "crazy" clients still persist), and if he can experience hope that the treatment will be successful. Once he agrees to such help, there must be help available. When a person is not greatly motivated for counseling in the first place, it is unlikely that he will retain even a mild willingness if he must wait while his name stays on a long waiting list. Once again, the church leader can be helpful at this point. If he is trained in counseling, he may be able to help the counselee deal with the problem without referral to outside resources. If referral seems wise, counseling in the church can often bridge the time gap until professional help is available.

*The third stage of secondary prevention is getting the necessary help for stopping and hopefully eliminating the developing abnormality.* The goal is not to remold the personality, but to work toward eliminating symptoms so the counselee can return to efficient functioning in his society, [16] and know how to handle recurring problems on his own.

An additional aspect of secondary prevention is helping those who have been released from mental hospitals, jails or other institutions to readjust to the community. Without this help, they sometimes slip back into their old ways. Halfway houses where former patients, addicts, alcoholics, or others live together to help each other, good foster homes, and other community assistance programs can often keep ex-patients on the road to recovery. The local mental health association can give information about these agencies and often can make practical suggestions for how the church can help.

## Mental Health and the Church

When the Joint Commission on Mental Illness and Health prepared its final report for the United States Congress in 1961, a number of "bold and challenging" recommendations were included. We need more research, the report concluded, more money for patient services, more professional and nonprofessional manpower, and more treatment facilities within the communities. Mental health, the report implied, is "everybody's business," from the highest government official to the lowliest citizen.

At the time of the report, clergymen outnumbered psychiatrists 35 to 1. For every person who went to a psychologist or psychiatrist for help, more than two people went to a pastor. Of those who went to pastors, about two-thirds reported that they had been helped, but less than

171

half who consulted professional counselors were satisfied. Obviously the church has an important role to play in the mental health movement, and perhaps "local churches and their pastors can potentially contribute more to the success of the mental health effort than any other...community group or agency." [17]

In the ten years that have elapsed since the Joint Commission's report, a number of churches have come to recognize their role in fostering mental health. Seminaries have introduced counseling programs, an increasing number of clergymen have taken training courses in pastoral psychology, and members of local congregations have become actively involved in the mental health movement. While establishing mental health in the community is not the church's primary role, if we believe that the Christian message has relevance to the needs of contemporary men, then we are responsible for bringing Christianity's resources to bear on the problems of those in our congregations and communities. There are at least ten practical ways in which church leaders can do this; all are consistent with biblical revelation and psychologically sound:*

*Introduce men to Jesus Christ.* The Bible does not promise that Christianity is a ticket to permanent mental health. The follower of Jesus Christ must bear a cross (Mt. 16:24; Mk. 8:34; 10:21; Lk. 9:23) and commit himself to a costly form of discipleship. Becoming a Christian often creates problems we could otherwise avoid. Why, then, should we encourage men and women to invite Christ into their lives? One reason is that by following Christ we have a challenging purpose in life (to follow Him), and a reason for living (Mt. 16:24-25; 2 Co. 5:15, 17; Gal. 2:20; Phil. 1:21). In addition, belief in Christ gives us "enduring faith" and a basis for the values that many psychologists consider to be so important. In times of

---

*In preparing these ten practical suggestions, I have drawn heavily on an excellent book by Howard J. Clinebell, Jr., entitled *Mental Health Through Christian Community.*

crises, Jesus Christ gives support and encouragement to those who depend on Him (Mt. 11:28-30). Indeed, the whole Christian life is one of fullness (Mk. 1:15; Jn. 10:10) and has been the experience of believers for centuries. Then, when we approach the end of life, we can face death knowing that there is eternal existence in a place prepared for those who have believed that Jesus Christ is the Son of God (Jn. 14:1-3; 3:16).

*Worship.* In the Old Testament, the worship of God was a central act in the life of the people. During His life on earth, Jesus reaffirmed the importance of worship both with His words (Mt. 4:10*b*; Jn. 4:23) and His example (Lk. 4:16). The early church worshiped together (Ac. 2:47); Paul encouraged believers to pray and give thanks (1 Ti.2:1); Peter and the writer of Hebrews instructed us to give praise (1 Pe. 2:9; Heb. 13:15); and the book of the Revelation indicates that worship will be a part of the future (4:10-11; 5:8-14; 7:9-12).

Worship is more than a divine commandment; however, it is an experience which encourages good mental health. For many, worship gives a feeling of oneness with others. As people sing in unison, pray together and draw near to God, they also draw closer to each other and feel less isolated. Worship that is reverent gives an awareness of God's presence, a renewed sense of trust, a feeling of superhuman strength, and an opportunity to sit quietly and reflect.

Too often worship in the local church is not a meaningful experience, but is instead a dull mechanical routine. In many churches—especially evangelical Protestant churches—there is considerable chatter (which we call "fellowship") before, after and sometimes during the services. The minister shows little sense of reverence and the people are deprived of an experience which could be spiritually uplifting and psychologically invigorating. Perhaps this is partly what Dr. Karl Menninger, the famous psychiatrist, had in mind recently when he said, "If only we could get clergymen

173

to appreciate what a marvellous opportunity for group therapy they let slip through their fingers every Sunday morning!"[18]

*Private devotions.* Here is another activity which was a vital part of the life of Jesus (Mk. 1:35; 6:46-47; Lk. 6:12) and is a must for every one of His followers (Ps. 46; 1 Th. 5:17; 1 Ti. 2:8; Jn. 5:39). Prayer gives us strength (1 Ch. 16:11; Lk. 18:1), wisdom (Mt. 7:7; Ja. 1:5); the ability to withstand temptations (Mt. 26:41),* joy (Jn. 16:24), the opportunity to express our feelings (Ja. 5:13); and the material things that we need and that God wants us to have (1 Jn. 5:14-15; Ja. 4:2-3; Mt. 21:22). Quiet meditation and study of the Scriptures give us knowledge, confidence and hope (2 Ti. 2:15; Jn. 5:39; Ro. 15:4).

In this age of hyperactivity and excessive busyness, men need to be still and get to know God (Ps. 46:10). Such a quiet time is another example of behavior which is of crucial importance, both spiritually and psychologically.

*Preaching.* Harry Emerson Fosdick once described preaching as "personal counseling on a group scale."[19] While this is a somewhat limited definition, it is true that the sermon can be a great opportunity for stimulating mental health. As he seeks to proclaim the Word of God, the preacher must show how the truths of the Bible apply to men's needs and everyday problems of living. The pulpit is no place for political discussions, airing of pet peeves, clichés, pompous irrelevant jargon, or messages which fail to relate to the needs of men. The sermon which Peter preached on the day of Pentecost (Ac. 2), is a good example of speaking to men's needs, showing the relevance of Scripture, and giving opportunity for men to make a practical response to the Word of God.

*Teaching.* The hour between 10 and 11 on Sunday morning has been called the "most wasted hour of the week." Thou-

---

*By withstanding temptation, we presumably also avoid the guilt which so often follows our yielding to temptation.

sands of youngsters are bored with Sunday school programs and become church dropouts as soon as they can get out from under parental pressure to attend. But the Christian education program is vital to the work of the church and can make a valuable contribution to mental health. But, to be effective, it must be reevaluated in many local congregations.

Numerous church members, denominational leaders, and specialists in the field of Christian education have been engaged in this evaluation, and as a result the church's teaching ministry has improved greatly. [20] To make a contribution to the mental health of church members, Christian educators can clearly teach the facts of one's faith, since this gives grounding in a belief system, and a sense of security in knowing where one stands; provide stimulation and challenge, since this is necessary for normal development; guide in the development of values and a philosophy of life; teach appreciation for the importance of consistent worship, meditation, prayer, and personal Bible study; discuss contemporary personal problems in the light of Scripture; consider such practical matters as one's vocation, family communication, relationships with the opposite sex, and marriage; provide opportunity for close interaction with other people; alert us to potential problems; and provide opportunity for counseling.*

*Stimulating healthy family life.* Most abnormal behavior can be traced back to an unhealthy family situation. Many research studies have shown that early experience in the home is of crucial importance and even wise King Solomon

---

*Clinebell in *Mental Health Through Christian Community* has listed signs which may indicate serious emotional problems in children: exaggerated aggressiveness, excessive daydreaming, inadequate peer relationships often linked with clinging dependency on adults, behavior which is childishly inappropriate to one's age, intense irrational fears, extreme guilt feelings, obsessive thoughts, compulsive actions, chronic lying or stealing, and psychotic symptoms.

recognized the importance of early training and discipline (Pr. 22:6; 13:24).

A healthy family is one which is characterized by love, mutual respect, communication, discipline, and religious training. In addition it is important that there be stimulation with such things as toys, books, activity, physical contacts, and verbal interaction with others. To foster this kind of environment, churches might consider the use of sermons that deal with the family, discussions or Bible-study groups which consider family relationships, premarital guidance, discussions with young married couples or young parents, and family counseling. It is also important that church activities not encourage family fragmentation. While graded Christian education classes are desirable, we must not split the church into so many specialized groups that there will be no opportunity for families to be together. To avoid this problem, some churches hold all of their weekly meetings on one night. Families participate together in a church dinner, and then the members disperse to their various age-group activities.

*Group interaction.* There are many things that a person can do alone, but being a Christian is not one of them. Jesus had a little band of twelve disciples whom He trained (Mt. 10) and sent forth as witnesses. The early church was a closely knit group that met together for study, fellowship, the "breaking of bread" and prayer (Ac. 2:42). The first missionary journeys were made by teams of men. Over the centuries it has become apparent that "the training of small groups has been a part of every major surge of spiritual vitality in the church." [21]

Within the past few years churches have shown a renewed interest in small groups. Christians have discovered that there is real spiritual growth when two or more people get together to pray, study, discuss, and share their personal needs or concerns. Group experience gives a feeling of "we-ness." It shows that somebody cares, and it gives us an opportunity to be concerned about others. In an age of great mobility, the church group gives people a "family" and a feeling of rootedness wherever they go.[22] It provides support in times of crises, friends in times of loneliness, and advice in times of indecision. In the small group we can learn how to relate to people and observe how others respond to us. Best of all, the Christian group draws us closer to God, for "where two or three are gathered together in my name," Jesus stated, "there am I in the midst of them" (Mt. 18:20).

Church groups are usually formed to fulfill one or more of the following tasks: study, prayer, work and service, mutual sharing of problems, and fellowship. While some of these tasks may be more therapeutic than others, all can contribute to better mental and spiritual health. It should be remembered, however, that people today are too busy to get involved in still another club or activity unless they can see that the group will have genuine relevance.[23] To insure this, the churchman should have a good understanding of how groups work as well as some skill in group leadership.

The following rules, suggested by I. Harris, an experienced group leader, may be helpful to those getting started:[24]

1. Start small. The ideal group size seems to be somewhere between eight and twelve people.

2. Be honest. People don't talk openly about themselves until they feel secure enough to do so, but it is easy to remain superficial and to hide our real feelings. We must learn, therefore, to be open with each other and to share our feelings *in a spirit of Christian love*.

3. Take leadership. The leadership of the group may shift from person to person, but often "natural" leaders will emerge. Sometimes it is helpful for the group to discuss who will lead or how leadership will be handled. In discussion groups it is sometimes best to let different people take leadership when they have something to contribute.

4. Give everyone a chance. Some people love to talk; others are shy. To get everyone involved, it is sometimes

wise to begin with some general questions: "What's your name?" "Tell us about your family," etc. Later more specific questions can be discussed, such as "When, if ever, in your life did God become more than a word?" [25]

5. Focus on spiritual growth and action. Some matters are too private to discuss openly, but it is often helpful to everyone if we can share some of our spiritual victories, failures and struggles.

6. Consider practical problems. Our personal frustrations and ambitions can often be shared in the group. We are then able to bear one another's burdens in Christian love.

7. Keep the beginner in mind. The newcomer should be made to feel welcome, but recognize also that he may be uncomfortable at the beginning. It is good not to push a person to talk until he feels ready to do so.

8. When groups become too large, subdivide.

9. Welcome pauses. At first we will be uncomfortable during periods of silence, but these can often be meaningful sharing and growing experiences.

10. Time and place are important. Usually it is best to meet regularly and in the same location. It is also advisable to set a time limit—perhaps an hour or ninety minutes—and to stop at the agreed time.

11. Make time for fellowship. Coffee, doughnuts, and casual conversation are often worthwhile, and this is a pleasant way to begin and/or end the meeting. It is important to listen, treat each other with love and respect, and keep the sessions flexible and informal. Such group experiences can bring new life to churches and new strength to believers.

*Service.* The gospel accounts indicate that Jesus spent much time in private communion with God, and that He devoted many hours to teaching His little group of disciples. But Jesus also was highly involved in service to others. He healed the sick, ministered to the needy, and preached from the Scriptures. Clearly He expects His followers to do likewise (Mt. 10:7-8; 28:19-20; Titus 3:8). A faith that does not lead men to do good works is a faith that is dead (Ja. 2:17-18).

The therapeutic value of service to others was discovered early by members of Alcoholics Anonymous who found that by helping others, they helped themselves. God has given men different gifts (Ro. 12; 1 Co. 12), and undoubtedly we have different responsibilities. We are called to difficult occupations and various places of work but no Christian is completely excused from service. The church, therefore, must encourage and mobilize the laborers. Guided by the Holy Spirit, our service will reach others and, in turn, help us both spiritually and psychologically.

*Support in crises.* In the United States and Canada it is considered bad manners to look closely at people in public. We are taught to respect the privacy of others and to avoid staring—even when we want very much to do so.[26] If other people are suffering or in need of help, we still pass by on the other side and pretend not to see. The psychotic is often dismissed as an "oddball" and rejected by his own family,[27] while patients who are dying find that their friends and even hospital personnel avoid the sickroom.[28] Apparently many of us are embarrassed and uncomfortable when in the presence of suffering and need.

But people who are facing crises need the help of others. The physically and mentally ill, the discouraged, bereaved, rejected, aged, and the families of such people all need support and encouragement. As followers of Christ who is always present when we are in need (Mt. 11:20, 28-30), Christians are failing in their duty if they neglect to minister to those facing the crises of life.

*Counseling.* One of the most direct contributions that the church can make to mental health is in counseling distressed people. In some communities the minister or other church leader may be the only counselor who is readily accessible; but even when other counselors are available, some people are reluctant to visit a psychologist. The minister is far less threatening and a great deal less expensive. The success of pastoral counseling depends in large measure on the church leader's training and familiarization with counseling procedures. This is the main thrust of the present book.

The story is told of the wonderful invention of Mr. Wahlstrom:

> It all started some years ago when Mr. Wahlstrom bought an old bombsight and took it apart just for the fun of it. When he began to put it together he found in his worskhop some parts of an old alarm clock. He became fascinated to see how he could add these to the bombsight. Thus it began, and in the years since he has been adding wheels, belts, bells, and cogs until today there are some ten thousand parts in Wahlstrom's wonder. When he throws the switch three thousand of them move while the whole apparatus revolves on a turntable. Bells ring, lights flash, and hundreds of wheels go round. It is an awesome sight! The only thing about it is Mr. Wahlstrom's wonder doesn't do anything. It just runs! Wheels within wheels, cogs with cogs. [29]

Some churches, and some church organizations, are like Wahlstrom's wonder. They run, but they don't really do anything. The practical steps listed above can do something to improve mental health and fulfill the requirements that Christ left for His church.

## SUMMARY

"Mental health is everybody's business" according to a widely used slogan, but everybody does not agree on what mental health actually is. Rather than search for a definition, it is more helpful to list some characteristics of the mentally healthy. These include social and emotional competence; satisfying interpersonal relations; periodic self-examination and insight; self-acceptance; self-confidence; a realistic approach to problems; freedom from internal conflict, intense feelings of insecurity, and paralyzing anxiety; a satisfying philosophy of life; and a capacity to love.

There are two general approaches to the prevention of abnormal behavior. First, we can prevent new disorders from ever getting started; and second, we can try to prevent existing problems from continuing or getting worse. The whole community must be responsible for this twofold preventive effort, but there are a number of practical ways in which the church can be involved. These include introducing men to Jesus Christ; holding reverent worship services; encouraging people to spend time in prayer, meditation and Bible study; presenting relevant sermons; running a well-planned Christian education program; stimulating healthy family life; encouraging group interaction; getting people involved in service, providing support in times of crisis; and counseling in times of need.

## NOTES

*Preface*

1. G. Gurin et al., *Americans View Their Mental Health.*
2. W. E. Oates, ed., *An Introduction to Pastoral Counseling*, p. vi.
3. Joint Commission on Mental Illness and Health, *Action for Mental Health.*

*Chapter 1*

1. J. W. Drakeford, *Counseling for Church Leaders.*
2. H. J. Clinebell, Jr., *Basic Types of Pastoral Counseling.*
3. R. F. Haase and D. J. DiMattia, "Proxemic Behavior," *Journal of Counseling Psychology* 17 (1970): 319-25.
4. A. Benjamin, *The Helping Interview.*
5. S. Freud, *The Problem of Lay-Analyses*, p. 11.
6. R. May, *The Art of Counseling.*
7. Benjamin.
8. J. S. Bonnell, *Psychology for Pastor and People*, p. 44.
9. C. M. Lowell, "Value Orientations—An Ethical Dilemma," *American Psychologist* 14 (1959): 687-93; Edith Weisskopf-Joelson, "Psychology and the Insights of Religion"; E. G. Williamson, "Value Orientation in Counseling" in *Humanistic Viewpoints in Psychology*, ed. F. T. Severin, pp. 359-77.
10. B. Shertzer and S. C. Stone, *Fundamentals of Counseling.*

11. D. Johnson, *Marriage Counseling: Theory and Practice*, p. vii.
12. Shertzer and Stone, p. 157.
13. C. M. Narramore, *The Psychology of Counseling*.
14. D. H. Blochér, *Developmental Counseling*.
15. D. Bonhoeffer, *Life Together*, pp. 87-88.
16. Drakeford.
17. Shertzer and Stone.
18. Benjamin.
19. Bonnell, p. 83.
20. E. H. Porter, Jr., *An Introduction to Therapeutic Counseling*.
21. D. F. Tweedie, *The Christian and the Couch*.
22. Narramore.
23. Drakeford, "The Budgeting of Time in Pastoral Counseling" in *An Introduction to Pastoral Counseling,* ed. W. E. Oates, pp. 96-107.
24. Benjamin.
25. Narramore, p. 29.
26. May, p. 173.
27. W. A. Clebsch and C. R. Jaekle, *Pastoral Care in Historical Perspective*, p. 68.


*Chapter 2*


1. R. N. Robertson, L. T. Maholick and D. S. Shapiro, "The Parish Minister as Counselor: A Dilemma and Challenge," *Pastoral Psychology* 20 (June 1969): 24-30.
2. W. E. Oates, "Making the Contact: Informal Pastoral Relationships" in *An Introduction to Pastoral Counseling*, pp. 69-80.
3. H. B. English and Ava C. English, *A Comprehensive Dictionary of Psychological and Psychoanalytical Terms*, p. 437.
4. W. A. Clebsch and C. R. Jaekle, *Pastoral Care in Historical Perspective*, p. 80.
5. H. J. Clinebell, Jr., *Basic Types of Pastoral Counseling*, p. 140.
6. Ibid.
7. E. Kübler-Ross, *On Death and Dying*.
8. O. H. Mowrer, *The Crisis in Psychiatry and Religion;* and J. W. Drakeford, *Counseling for Church Leaders*.
9. J. Dollard and N. E. Miller, *Personality and Psychotherapy*; and R. Dayringer, "A Learning-Theory Approach to Pastoral Counseling," *Pastoral Psychology* 20 (Mar. 1969): 39-43.
10. S. Freud, *Civilization and Its Discontents*, p. 26.
11. Clinebell, p. 147.
12. W. B. Oglesby, Jr., *Referral in Pastoral Counseling*.
13. S. Hiltner, *Pastoral Counseling*, pp. 89-90.
14. Clinebell, pp. 82-92.
15. C. Reid, *Groups Alive— Church Alive*
16. K. Miller, *A Second Touch*, p. 142.
17. Clinebell; and J. W. Knowles, *Group Counseling*.


*Chapter 3*


1. Joint Commission on Mental Illness and Health, *Action for Mental Health*.
2. M. P. Strommen, *Profiles of Church Youth*; R. B. Zuck and G. A. Getz, *Christian Youth: An In-Depth Study*.
3. H. J. Clinebell, Jr., *Basic Types of Pastoral Counseling*, p. 96.

4. L. M. Terman, *Psychological Factors in Marital Happiness.*
5. J. K. Morris, *Premarital Counseling: A Manual for Ministers;* and R. L. Dicks, *Premarital Guidance.*
6. K. R. Mitchell, "Reinterpreting the Purpose of Premarital Counseling," *Pastoral Psychology* 18 (Oct. 1967): 18-24.
7. J. R. Udry, *The Social Context of Marriage*; and J. C. Coleman, *Psychology and Effective Behavior.*
8. Ibid.
9. R. O. Blood, Jr., *Marriage*; J. Nederhood, *Too Early to Marry*; and J. C. Coleman, *Psychology and Effective Behavior.*
10. D. L. Womble, *Foundations for Marriage and Family Relations.*
11. P. H. Landis, *Making the Most of Marriage.*
12. Blood.
13. J. T. Landis, "Adjustments After Marriage," *Marriage and Family Living* 9 (1947): 32-34.
14. D. Mace, *Marriage, the Art of Lasting Love,* pp. 46-47.
15. Womble.
16. H. J. Miles, *Sexual Happiness in Marriage.*
17. S. B. Babbage, *Sex and Sanity*; and B. L. Smith, "Till Death Us Do Part?" *Christianity Today* 14 (Jan. 16, 1970): 5-10.
18. Helpful books include: S. A. Lewin and J. Gilmore, *Sex Without Fear*; H. J. Miles, *Sexual Happiness in Marriage;* D. H. Small, *Design for Christian Marriage*; and R. B. Thieme, Jr., *The Biblical View of Sex, Love and Marriage.*
19. Morris.
20. W. E. Oates, *Premarital Pastoral Care and Counseling*; and Morris.
21. H. E. Terkelsen, *Counseling the Unwed Mother*; and T. Howard, "What About Unwed Mothers?" *Christianity Today* 14 (Mar. 13, 1970): 11-12.
22. A. L. Rutledge, *Pre-marital Counseling.*
23. Morris.
24. Clinebell, p. 98.
25. A. D. Bell, *The Family in Dialogue.*
26. Blood.
27. W. L. Carrington, *The Healing of Marriage.*
28. R. Athanasious et al., "Sex," *Psychology Today* 4 (July 1970).
29. Clinebell, p. 98.
30. W. C. Ellzey, "Education for the Newly Married," *Pastoral Psychology* 19 (May 1968): 21-26.
31. G. V. Ramsey, "Group Marriage Counseling for Normal Young Marrieds," *Pastoral Psychology* 13 (Mar. 1962): 30-34.
32. A. H. Jacobson, "Conflict of Attitudes Toward the Roles of the Husband and Wife in Marriage," *American Sociological Review* 17 (1952): 146-50.
33. Blood.
34. W. Kaufman, "Some Emotional Uses of Money," *Pastoral Psychology* 16 (Apr. 1965): 43-56.
35. R. L. Hudson, *Marital Counseling.*
36. Blood.
37. Thieme.
38. V. Satir, *Cojoint Family Therapy.*
39. Buker.

*Chapter 4*

1. Vance Packard, *Status Seekers.*
2. M. Rosenburg, *Occupations and Values.*
3. H. Weits,\"Guidance as Behavioral Change," *American Personnel and Guidance Journal* (Mar. 1961), pp. 558-59.
4. R. B. Hackman, "Vocational Counseling with Adolescents" in *Understanding Adolescence,* ed. J. F. Adams, p. 384.
5. R. A. Kalish, *The Psychology of Human Behavior.*
6. L. J. Bischof, *Adult Psychology.*
7. J. H. Dickerson, "The Pastor's Role with Job-Related Problems," *Pastoral Psychology* 12 (Sept. 1961): 29-30.
8. A. Richardson, *The Biblical Doctrine of Work.*
9. G. R. Collins, *Man in Transition,* chap. 5.
10. Wilma Donahue et al., "Retirement: The Emerging Social Pattern" in *Handbook of Social Gerontology,* ed. C. Tibbits.
11. E. C. Thoroman, *The Vocational Counseling of Adults and Young People.*
12. D. E. Johnson, "A Depressive Retirement Syndrome," *Geriatrics* 13 (1958): 314-19.
13. W. E. Thompson, "Pre-retirement Anticipation and Adjustment in Retirement," *Journal of Social Issues* 14, no. 2 (1958): 35-45.
14. J. E. Birren, *The Psychology of Aging;* and R. McFarland and B. O'Doherty, "Work and Occupational Skills" in *Handbook of Aging and the Individual,* ed. J. B. Birren.
15. P. McGinley, *Sixpence in Her Shoe,* pp. 5-6, 2.
16. Bischof.
17. C. F. Kemp, *The Pastor and Vocational Counseling.*
18. Ibid.
19. G. E. Whitlock, "The Role of the Minister in Vocational Counseling," *Pastoral Psychology* 12 (Sept. 1961): 14-22.
20. M. Bittner, "Educational and Vocational Counseling," *The Pastor's Manual* (Fall, 1965), pp. 8-19.


*Chapter 5*

1. P. Meehl, "Wanted—A Good Cookbook," *American Psychologist* 11 (1956): 263-72.
2. E. E. Bruder, "The Pastoral Ministry to the Mentally Ill," *Pastoral Psychology* 17 (1966): 23-27.
3. P. B. Maves, ed., *The Church and Mental Health,* p. 189.
4. J. L. Christenson, *The Pastor's Counseling Handbook.*
5. H. J. Clinebell, Jr., *Mental Health Through Christian Community.*
6. D. C. Houts, "Ministering to the Family Dimensions of Illness," *Pastoral Psychology* 18 (Nov. 1967): 36-44.
7. J. Robertson, *Young Children in Hospital;* and J. Bowlby, "Grief and Mourning in Infancy and Early Childhood," *Psychoanalytic Study of the Child* 15 (1960): 9-52.
8. J. E. Kilgore, *Pastoral Care of the Hospitalized Child.*
9. J. T. Meigs, "Pastoral Care of Parents of Children with Cancer" in W. E. Oates and A. D. Lester, *Pastoral Care in Crucial Human Situations;* and L. Goldfogel,

"Working with the Parent of a Dying Child," *American Journal of Nursing* 70 (Aug. 1970): 1675-79.

10. T. Howard, "What About Unwed Mothers?" *Christianity Today* 14 (Mar. 13, 1970): 11-12.

11. E. Kübler-Ross, *On Death and Dying.*

12. Ibid, p. 100.

13. Ibid., p. 123.

14. Ibid.; and T. Shea, "New Seminar Helps Take the Sting out of Death," *National Observer* (Jan. 5, 1970). p. 22.

15. J. Hinton, *Dying.*

16. I. L. Janis et al., *Personality and Persuasibility.*

17. W. F. Rogers, "The Pastor's Work with Grief," *Pastoral Psychology* 14 (Sept. 1963): 19-26.

18. E. Lindemann, "Symptomatology and Management of Acute Grief," *The American Journal of Psychiatry* 101 (Sept. 1944): 141-48.

19. C. C. Bachmann, *Ministering to the Grief Sufferer*; and E. N. Jackson, *For the Living.*

20. G. Gorer, *Death, Grief, and Mourning.*

21. J. Mitford, *The American Way of Death*; and R. J. Becker, "Funeral—Memorial or Burial?" *Pastoral Psychology* 15 (Apr. 1964): 50-53.

22. R. J. Hastings, "Are Funerals Dying Out?" *Christianity Today* 13 (Nov. 22, 1968): 13-14.

23. Gorer, p. 121.

24. W. M. Lamers, Jr., "Death, Grief, Mourning, the Funeral and the Child";

E. N. Jackson, *Telling a Child About Death*; and S. Wolff, *Children Under Stress.*

25. A. L. Goddard, "Churches Do Care," *Pastoral Psychology* 16 (June 1965): 23-28.

26. T. L. Duncan, *Understanding and Helping the Narcotic Addict.*

27. B. J. Soules, "Thalidomide Victims in a Rehabilitation Center," *American Journal of Nursing* 66 (Sept. 1966): 2023-26.

28. V. Kreyer, "Feelings of Handicapped Individuals," *Pastoral Psychology* 16 (June 1965): 41-44.

29. S. L. Fink, "Crisis and Motivation: A Theoretical Model," *Archives of Physical Medicine and Rehabilitation* 48 (Nov. 1967).

30. E. F. Proelss, "Ministering to the Physically Disabled Person," *Pastoral Psychology* 16 (June 1965): 8-22, 66.

31. V. Kreyer, "Feelings of Handicapped Individuals," *Pastoral Psychology* 16 (June 1965): 43-44.

32. Tom Skinner, *Black and Free.*

33. W. H. Grier and P. M. Cobb, *Black Rage.*


*Chapter 6*


1. Joint Commission on Mental Illness and Health, *Action for Mental Health.*

2. H. A. Bowman, "The Nature of Mental Health" in *Understanding Mental Health*, ed. R. I. Sutherland and B. K. Smith, p. 33.

3. H. J. Clinebell, Jr., *Mental Health Through Christian Community*, p. 17.

4. J. O. Kempson, "Beyond Cliche Concepts," *Pastoral Psychology* 20 (May 1969): 6.

5. Thomas Szasz, "The Myth of Mental Illness," *American Psychologist* 15 (1960): 118.

6. M. Jahoda, *Current Concepts of Positive Mental Health*, pp. 13-14, as quoted by Clinebell.

7. Erich Fromm, *The Sane Society.*

8. J. R. Strange, *Abnormal Psychology: Understanding Behavior Disorders*.
9. S. M. Jourard, *The Transparent Self*.
10. Bowman.
11. Fromm, *Man for Himself*, pp. 97-98.
12. Fromm, *The Art of Loving*.
13. G. Caplan, "Prevention of Mental Disorders" in *The Encyclopedia of Mental Health* 5:1561.
14. Ibid.
15. Ibid.
16. Caplan.
17. E. E. Bruder, "A Time of Challenge," *Pastoral Psychology* 16 (May 1965): 6.
18. Mary Harrington Hall, "An Interview with Karl Menninger," *Psychology Today* 2 (Feb. 1969): 63.
19. H. E. Fosdick, Interview on NBC-TV (May 10, 1959), as quoted by Clinebell, p. 77.
20. W. J. Peterson, "What's the Future of the Sunday School?" *Eternity* 19 (Oct. 1968): 11-14.
21. Clinebell, pp. 151-52.
22. H. A. Burch, "The Church and Its Pastor: Community Agents," *Pastoral Psychology* 17 (1966): 23-27.
23. E. Wismer, "Small Groups and Church Renewal," *Pastoral Psychology* 18 (Mar. 1967): 7-13.
24. I. Harris, "Finding a Handle" in B. Larson et al., *Groups that Work*, pp. 11-15.
25. K. Miller, "Behind Our Masks" in ibid., pp. 16-19.
26. J. M. Darley and B. Latané, "When Will People Help in a Crisis?" *Psychology Today* 2 (Dec. 1968): 54-57, 70-71.
27. Joint Commission.
28. E. Kübler-Ross, *On Death and Dying*.
29. G. E. Bartlett, "The Minister: Pastor or Promoter," *Pastoral Psychology* 13 (Sept. 1957).

# SUGGESTIONS FOR FURTHER READING

### Chapter 1

W. E. Hulme's *How to Start Counseling* is, as the title implies, a good place to begin one's extra reading in this subject. Then, it would be wise to look at these three books: A. Benjamin's *The Helping Interview*\* is not written specifically for church leaders, but it is a clear, nontechnical presentation which would be helpful for any counselor. S. R. Laycock's *Pastoral Counseling for Mental Health*\* is a brief but concise source of information. Much older, but still relevant is R. May's *The Art of Counseling*.\* W. E. Crane's *Where God Comes In* discusses counseling from a uniquely Christian perspective.

S. Hiltner's *The Counselor in Counseling*\* is a good discussion of counselor characteristics. J. W. Drakeford's *Counseling for Church Leaders* and C. M. Narramore's *The Psychology of Counseling* are elementary introductions to counseling. For a more extensive treatment of the subject, see L. M. Brammer and E. L. Shostrom's *Therapeutic Psychology* or B. Shertzer and S. C. Stone's *Fundamentals of Counseling*.

## Chapter 2

The material in this chapter is discussed in more detail in an excellent book by H. J. Clinebell, Jr., entitled *Basic Types of Pastoral Counseling*. A book edited by W. E. Oates, *An Introduction to Pastoral Counseling*, is also relevant, as is D. L. Farnsworth and F. J. Braceland's *Psychiatry, the Clergy and Pastoral Counseling*\* and W. E. Oates and A. D. Lester's *Pastoral Care in Crucial Human Situations*. J. Dollard and N. E. Miller's *Personality and Psychotherapy*\* is a readable and not too technical discussion of the learning approach to counseling. For a further consideration of referral counseling, see the book by W. B. Oglesby, Jr., *Referral in Pastoral Counseling*. Group counseling in the church is discussed in J. W. Knowles' *Group Counseling*\*, R. C. Leslie's *Sharing Groups in the Church* and in C. Reid's *Group Alive—Church Alive*. O. H. Mowrer's *The New Group Therapy*\*, and J. W. Drakeford's *Integrity Therapy* are not specifically geared to religious counseling, but they say a great deal about it and would be helpful reading for church leaders. The layman's role is considered in Drakeford's *Counseling for Church Leaders* and in the June, 1971, issue of *Pastoral Psychology*.

## Chapter 3

So many books have been written in the area of marriage and family guidance that it is difficult to select a few for suggested reading. Once again, the Successful Pastoral Counseling Series has several relevant titles, including R. L. Dicks, *Premarital Guidance*\*; R. L. Hudson, *Marital Counseling*\*; R. J. Becker, *Family Pastoral Care*\*; W. T. Bassett, *Counseling the Childless Couple*\*; and H. E. Terkelsen, *Counseling the Unwed Mother*.\*

J. K. Morris, *Premarital Counseling: A Manual for Ministers* is a good introduction, and so is the little book by W. E. Oates, *Premarital Pastoral Care and Counseling*.\* Of the several books available on marriage counseling, the church leader could especially profit from C. W. Stewart's *The Minister as Marriage Counselor* and D. Johnson's *Marriage Counseling: Theory and Practice*.

More sophisticated treatments of the material in this chapter include B. N. Ard and C. C. Ard, *Handbook of Marriage Counseling*; M. Ackerman, *Treating the Troubled Family*; R. O. Blood, Jr., *Marriage*; and N. W. Bell and E. E. Vogel, eds., *A Modern Introduction to the Family*. None of these has any unique Christian perspective, although Blood's book is sympathetic to religion.

For the church lending library, there is value in having W. E. Hulme's *Building a Christian Marriage*; R. B. Thieme's *The Biblical View of Sex, Love and Marriage*; Evelyn M. Duvall's *Why Wait Till Marriage?* and *Inlaws: Pro and Con*; W. Fitch's *Christian Perspectives on Sex and Marriage*\*; and the two books by D. H. Small, *Design for Christian Marriage* and *After You've Said I Do*. For couples approaching marriage, S. A. Lewin and J. Gilmore's *Sex Without Fear* is a good survey of physiology, while H. J. Miles' *Sexual Happiness in Marriage*\* is a down-to-earth discussion of marital sex in general. *The Intimate Marriage* by H. J. Clinebell, Jr., and C. H. Clinebell is an excellent volume designed to be read by couples or groups of married couples who want to make their marriages better.

## Chapter 4

Books on pastoral counseling tend to ignore or say very little about vocational counseling. Two exceptions are C. F. Kemp's *The Pastor and Vocational Counseling*, and S. Southard's *Counseling for Church Vocations*. Also of value is the September, 1961, issue of *Pastoral Psychology* magazine\* which is devoted entirely to articles on "The church, the minister, and vocational counseling." E. C. Thoroman's *The Vocational Counseling of Adults and Young Adults* is more recent although it makes no special reference to vocational counseling in the church. For a more sophisticated treatment of vocational counseling as a profession, see B. Shertzer and S. C. Stone's *Fundamentals of Guidance*.

\*Available in paperback editions.

The third volume in the Psychology for Church Leaders Series, *Fractured Personalities* (1972)\* has been written to help the reader understand mental illness. E. E. Bruder's *Ministering to Deeply Troubled People*\* gives some practical help in counseling with emotionally disturbed people and their families.

J. E. Kilgore's *Pastoral Care of the Hospitalized Child* and C. J. Scherzer's *Ministering to the Physically Sick*\* give an introduction to counseling with the physically ill, although Scherzer's book has what some will consider an overabundance of poems and prayers.

Elizabeth Kübler-Ross' *On Death and Dying*\* is a widely acclaimed book on terminal illness. Less readable is J. Hinton's *Dying* and Scherzer's *Ministering to the Dying*.\*

A number of books discuss grief. Catherine Marshall's *To Live Again*\* and G. Kooiman's *When Death Takes a Father*\* are helpful autobiographical accounts. C. C. Bachmann's *Ministering to the Grief Sufferer*\* is worth reading, as are the books by Edgar Jackson. Although these sometimes sound like they are written as a defense of morticians, the church leader can learn much from E. N. Jackson's *Understanding Grief, For the Living*\*, and *Telling a Child About Death*. Joseph Bayly's *The View from a Hearse*\* is a readable discussion of death from a Christian perspective, written by a man who has lost three sons.

An entire issue of *Pastoral Psychology*\* (June, 1965) has been devoted to "The Church and the Physically Handicapped." B. A. Wright's *Physical Disability— A Psychological Approach* could be a helpful reference book.

*Chapter 6*

It is difficult to find good books on mental health. R. I. Sutherland and B. K. Smith's *Understanding Mental Health*\* is readable and contains a number of interesting chapters; R. V. McCann's *The Churches and Mental Health* is a report of a national survey; while O. H. Mowrer's *Morality and Mental Health* is a large volume which contains a number of articles that would be of interest to church leaders. For discussion of the role of the local church in the prevention of abnormal behavior, there is no better book than *Mental Health Through Christian Community* by H. J. Clinebell, Jr.

The role of small groups in the church is considered in the June, 1964, and March, 1967, issues of *Pastoral Psychology*.\* Also helpful are B. Larson et. al., *Groups that Work*\*, J. L. Casteel, ed., *Spiritual Renewal Through Personal Groups*, R. C. Leslie, *Sharing Groups in the Church*\*, and C. Reid, *Groups Alive—Church Alive*. A.L. Teikmanis, *Preaching and Pastoral Care*\* shows how preaching can contribute to mental health.

\*Available in paperback editions.

# BIBLIOGRAPHY

Ackerman, M. *Treating the Troubled Family.* New York: Basic Books, 1966.

Ard, B. N. and Ard, C. C., eds. *Handbook of Marriage Counseling.* Palo Alto, Calif.: Science and Behavior Books, 1969.

Athanasious, et al.

Babbage, S. B. *Christianity and Sex.* Chicago: Inter-Varsity, 1963.

—————. *Sex and Sanity: A Christian View of Sexual Morality.* Philadelphia: Westminster, 1967.

Bachmann, C. C. *Ministering to the Grief Sufferer.* Philadelphia: Fortress, 1967.

Baer, M. F. and Roeber, E. S. *Occupational Information: The Dynamics of Its Nature and Use.* Chicago: Science Research Associates, 1964.

Bartlett, G. E. "The Minister: Pastor or Promoter," *Pastoral Psychology* 13 (Sept. 1957).

Bassett, W. T. *Counseling the Childless Couple.* Philadelphia: Fortress, 1963.

Bayly, Joseph T. *The View from a Hearse.* Elgin, Ill.: Cook, 1969.

—————. *Family Pastoral Care.* Englewood Cliffs, N. J.: Prentice-Hall, 1968.

Becker, R. J. "Funeral—Memorial or Burial?" *Pastoral Psychology* 15 (Apr. 1964): 50-53.

Bell, A. D. *The Family in Dialogue.* Rev. ed. Grand Rapids: Zondervan, 1970.

Bell, N. W. and Vogel, E. F., eds. *A Modern Introduction to the Family.* Rev. ed. New York: Free, 1968.

Benjamin, A. *The Helping Interview.* Boston: Houghton Mifflin, 1969.

Birren, J. E. *The Psychology of Aging.* Englewood Cliffs, N. J.: Prentice-Hall, 1964.

Bischof, L. J. *Adult Psychology.* New York: Harper & Row, 1969.

Bittner, M. "Educational and Vocational Counseling," *The Pastor's Manual* (Fall, 1965), pp. 8-19.

Blocher, D. H. *Developmental Counseling.* New York: Ronald, 1966.

Blood, R. O., Jr. *Marriage.* Glencoe, Ill.: Free, 1962.

Boneau, C. A.; Golann, S. E. and Johnson, M. M. *A Career in Psychology.* Washington, D. C.: American Psychological Assn., 1970. Booklet.

Bonhoeffer, D. *Life Together.* London: SCM, 1954.

Bonnell, J. S. *Psychology for Pastor and People.* New York: Harper, 1948.

Bowlby, J. "Grief and Mourning in Infancy and Early Childhood," *Psychoanalytic Study of the Child* 15 (1960): 9-52.

Bowman, H. A. "The Nature of Mental Health" in *Understanding Mental Health,* ed. R. I. Sutherland and B. K. Smith. Princeton, N. J.: Van Nostrand, 1965, pp. 33-39.

Brammer, L. M. and Shostrom, E. L. *Therapeutic Psychology.* Englewood Cliffs, N. J.: Prentice-Hall, 1968.

Brister, C. W., ed. "Training Lay People for Pastoral Care," *Pastoral Psychology* 22, no. 215 (June 1971), entire issue.

Bruder, E. E. *Ministering to Deeply Troubled People.* Philadelphia: Fortress, 1964.

—————. "The Pastoral Ministry to the Mentally Ill," *Pastoral Psychology* 17 (1966): 23-27.

—————. "A Time of Challenge," *Pastoral Psychology* 16 (May 1965): 5-7.

Burch, H. A. "The Church and Its Pastor: Community Agents," *Pastoral Psychology* 20 (May 1969): 19-24.

Caplan, G. "Prevention of Mental Disorders" in *The Encyclopedia of Mental Health,* vol. 5, ed. A. Deutsch and H. Fishman. New York: Franklin Watts, 1963, pp. 1556-66.

Carrington, W. L. *The Healing of Marriage: A Practical Handbook of Marriage Counseling.* Great Neck, N.Y.: Channel, 1961.

Casteel, J. L., ed. *Spiritual Renewal Through Personal Groups.* New York: Association, 1957.

Christensen, J. L. *The Pastor's Counseling Handbook.* Westwood, N. J.: Revell, 1963.

Clebsch, W. A. and Jaekle, C. R. *Pastoral Care in Historical Perspective.* Englewood Cliffs, N.J.: Prentice-Hall, 1964.

Clinebell, H. J., Jr. *Mental Health Through Christian Community.* New York: Abingdon, 1965.

—————. *Basic Types of Pastoral Counseling.* Nashville: Abingdon, 1966.

Clinebell, H. J., Jr. and Clinebell, C. H. *The Intimate Marriage.* New York: Harper & Row, 1970.

Coleman, J. C. *Psychology and Effective Behavior.* Glenview, Ill.: Scott, Foresman, 1969.

Collins, G. R. *Fractured Personalities.* Carol Stream, Ill.: Creation House, 1972.

—————. *Living in Peace: The Psychology of Interpersonal Relations.* Wheaton, Ill.: Key, 1970.

—————. "The Pastor and His Counseling Service" in W. Kerr, *The Minister's Research Service.* Wheaton, Ill.: Tyndale, 1970, pp. 131-44.

Crane, W. E. *Where God Comes In: The Divine Plus in Counseling.* Waco, Tex.: Word, 1970.

Darley, J. M. and Latané, B. "When Will People Help in a Crisis?" *Psychology Today* 2 (Dec. 1968): 54-57, 70-71.

Dayringer, R. "A Learning-Theory Approach to Pastoral Counseling," *Pastoral Psychology* 20 (Mar. 1969): 39-43.

Dickerson, J. H. "The Pastor's Role with Job-Related Problems," *Pastoral Psychology* 12 (Sept. 1961): 29-36.

Dicks, R. L. *Premarital Guidance.* Philadelphia: Fortress, 1963.

Dollard, J. and Miller, N. E. *Personality and Psychotherapy.* New York: McGraw-Hill, 1950.

Donahue, Wilma; Orbach, H. L. and Pollak, O. "Retirement: The Emerging Social Pattern" in *Handbook of Social Gerontology,* ed. C. Tibbits. Chicago: U. Chicago, 1960, pp. 330-406.

Drakeford, J. W. "The Budgeting of Time in Pastoral Counseling" in *An Introduction to Pastoral Counseling,* ed. W. E. Oates. Nashville: Broadman, 1959, pp. 96-107.

—————. *Counseling for Church Leaders.* Nashville: Broadman, 1961.

—————. *Integrity Therapy.* Nashville: Broadman, 1967.

Duncan, T. L. *Understanding and Helping the Narcotic Addict.* Philadelphia: Fortress, 1968.

Duvall, Evelyn M. *Why Wait Till Marriage?* New York: Association, 1965.

—————. *In-Laws: Pro and Con.* New York: Association, 1964.

Ellzey, W. C. "Education for the Newly Married," *Pastoral Psychology* 19 (May 1968): 21-26.

English, H. B. and English, Ava C. *A Comprehensive Dictionary of Psychological and Psychoanalytical Terms.* New York: Longmans, Green, 1958.

Farnsworth, D. L. and Braceland, F. J. *Psychiatry, the Clergy and Pastoral Counseling,* 1969.

Fink, S. L. "Crisis and Motivation: A Theoretical Model," *Archives of Physical Medicine and Rehabilitation* 48 (Nov. 1967).

Fitch, W. *Christian Perspectives on Sex and Marriage.* Grand Rapids: Eerdmans, 1971.

Fosdick, H. E. Interview on NBC-TV (May 10, 1959), as quoted by H. J. Clinebell, Jr., *Mental Health Through Christian Community.* New York: Abingdon, 1965, p. 77.

Freud, S. *Civilization and Its Discontents.* London: Hogarth, 1953.

—————. *The Problem of Lay-Analyses.* Trans. A. Paul Maerker-Brauden. New York: Bretano, 1928.

Fromm, Erich. *The Art of Loving.* New York: Harper & Row, 1956.

—————. *Man for Himself.* New York: Rinehart, 1947.

—————. *The Sane Society.* New York: Rinehart, 1955.

Goddard, A. L. "Churches Do Care," *Pastoral Psychology* 16 (June 1965): 23-28.

Goldfogel, L. "Working with the Parent of a Dying Child," *American Journal of Nursing* 70 (Aug. 1970): 1675-79.

Goodwin, H. M. and Mudd, E. H. "Marriage Counseling: Methods and Goals" in *Handbook of Marriage Counseling,* ed. B. N. Ard, Jr., and C. C. Ard. Palo Alto Calif.: Science and Behavior Books, 1969, pp. 93-105.

Gorer, G. *Death, Grief and Mourning.* Garden City, N. Y.: Doubleday Anchor Books, 1965.

Greene, B. L. *The Psychotherapies of Marital Disharmony.* New York: Free, 1965.

Grier, W. H. and Cobbs, P. M. *Black Rage.* New York: Basic Books, 1968.

Gurin, G.; Veroff, J. and Feld, S. *Americans View Their Mental Health: A Nationwide Survey.* New York: Basic Books, 1960.

Haase, R. F. and DiMattia, D. J. "Proxemic Behavior: Counselor, Administrator, and Client Preference for Seating Arrangement and Dyadic Interaction," *Journal of Counseling Psychology* 17 (1970): 319-25.

Hackman, R. B. "Vocational Counseling with Adolescents" in *Understanding Adolescence: Current Developments in Adolescent Psychology,* ed. J. F. Adams. Boston: Allyn & Bacon, 1968, pp. 361-86.

Hall, Mary Harrington. "An Interview with Karl Menninger," *Psychology Today* 2 (Feb. 1969): 56-63.

Harris, I. "Finding a Handle" in B. Larson et al. *Groups that Work.* Grand Rapids: Zondervan, 1967, pp. 11-15.

Hastings, R. J. "Are Funerals Dying Out?" *Christianity Today* 13 (Nov. 22, 1968): 13-14.

Hiltner, S. *Pastoral Counseling.* Nashville: Abingdon, 1949.

—————. *The Counselor in Counseling.* Nashville: Abingdon, 1952.

Hinton, J. *Dying.* Baltimore: Penguin Books, 1967.

Houts, D. C. "Ministering to the Family Dimensions of Illness," *Pastoral Psychology* (Nov. 1967), pp. 36-44.

Howard, T. "The Human Experience of Death," *Christianity Today* 14 (Nov. 21, 1969): 6-8.

—————. "What About Unwed Mothers?" *Christianity Today* 14 (Mar. 13, 1970): 11-12.

Hudson, R. L. *Marital Counseling.* Philadelphia: Fortress, 1963.

Hulme, W. E. *Building a Christian Marriage.* Englewood Cliffs, N. J.: Prentice-Hall, 1965.

—————. *How to Start Counseling.* New York: Abingdon, 1955.

Jackson, E. N. *For the Living.* Des Moines, Ia.: Channel, 1963.

—————. *Telling a Child About Death.* New York: Channel, 1965.

—————. *Understanding Grief.* New York: Abingdon, 1957.

191

Jacobson, A. H. "Conflict of Attitudes Toward the Roles of the Husband and Wife in Marriage," *American Sociological Review* 17 (1952): 146-50.

Jahoda, M. *Current Concepts of Positive Mental Health.* New York: Basic Books, 1958.

Janis, I. L. et al. *Personality and Persuasibility.* New Haven: Yale U., 1959.

Johnson, D. E. "A Depressive Retirement Syndrome," *Geriatrics* 13 (1958): 314-19.

Johnson, D. *Marriage Counseling: Theory and Practice.* Englewood Cliffs, N. J.: Prentice-Hall, 1961.

Joint Commission on Mental Illness and Health. *Action for Mental Health: Final Report of the Joint Commission on Mental Illness and Health.* New York: Science Editions, 1961.

Jourard, S. M. *The Transparent Self.* Rev. ed. Princeton, N. J.: Van Nostrand, 1971.

Kalish, R. A. *The Psychology of Human Behavior*, Belmont, Calif.: Wadworth, 1966.

Kaufman, W. "Some Emotional Uses of Money," *Pastoral Psychology* 16 (Apr. 1965): 43-56.

Kemp, C. F. *The Pastor and Vocational Counseling.* St. Louis: Bethany, 1961.

Kempson, J. O. "Beyond Cliché Concepts," *Pastoral Psychology* 20 (May 1969): 5-8.

Kilgore, J.E. *Pastoral Care of the Hospitalized Child.* New York: Exposition, 1968.

Kirkendall, L. A. *Marriage and Family Relations: A Reading and Study Guide for Students.* 3d ed. Dubuque, Ia.: Brown, 1965.

Knowles, J. W. *Group Counseling.* Philadelphia: Fortress, 1964.

Kooiman, G. *When Death Takes a Father.* Grand Rapids: Baker, 1968.

Kreyer, V. "Feelings of Handicapped Individuals," *Pastoral Psychology* 16 (June 1965): 41-44.

Kübler-Ross, E. *On Death and Dying.* New York: Macmillan, 1969.

Lamers, W. M., Jr. "Death, Grief, Mourning, the Funeral and the Child." Illustrated lecture presented to the National Assn., Funeral Directors, Chicago (Nov. 1, 1965).

Landis, J. T. "Adjustments After Marriage," *Marriage and Family Living* 9 (1947): 32-34.

Landis, P. H. *Making the Most of Marriage.* 3d ed. New York: Appleton-Century-Crofts, 1965.

Larson, B. et al. *Groups that Work.* Grand Rapids: Zondervan, 1967.

Laycock, S. R. *Pastoral Counseling for Mental Health.* Nashville: Abingdon, 1961.

Leslie, R. C. *Sharing Groups in the Church.* Nashville: Abingdon, 1971.

Lewin, S. A. and Gilmore, J. *Sex Without Fear.* 2d rev. ed. New York: Medical Research Press, 1965.

Lindemann, E. "Symptomatology and Management of Acute Grief," *The American Journal of Psychiatry* 101 (Sept. 1944): 141-48.

Lowe, C. M. "Value Orientations—An Ethical Dilemma," *American Psychologist* 14 (1959): 687-93.

Mace, D. *Marriage, the Art of Lasting Love.* Garden City, N. Y.: Doubleday, 1952.

Marshall, C. *To Live Again.* New York: McGraw-Hill, 1957.

Maves, P. B., ed. *The Church and Mental Health.* New York: Scribner, 1953.

May, R. *The Art of Counseling.* New York: Abingdon, 1939.

McCann, R. V. *The Churches and Mental Health.* New York: Basic Books, 1962.

McFarland, R. and O'Doherty, B. "Work and Occupational Skills" in *Handbook of Aging and the Individual*, ed. J. B. Birren. Chicago: U. Chicago, 1959, pp. 452-500.

McGinley, P. *Sixpence in Her Shoe*. New York: Macmillan, 1964.

Meehl, P. "Wanted—A Good Cookbook," *American Psychologist* 11 (1956): 263-72.

Meigs, J. T. "Pastoral Care of Parents of Children with Cancer" in W. E. Oates and A. D. Lester, *Pastoral Care in Crucial Human Situations*. Valley Forge, Pa.: Judson, 1969, pp. 62-89.

Miles, H. J. *Sexual Happiness in Marriage: A Christian Interpretation of Sexual Adjustment in Marriage*. Grand Rapids: Zondervan, 1967.

Miller, K. "Behind Our Masks" in B. Larson et al., *Groups that Work*. Grand Rapids: Zondervan, 1967, pp. 16-19.

— — — — . *A Second Touch*. Waco, Tex.: Word, 1967.

Mitchell, K. R. "Reinterpreting the Purpose of Premarital Counseling," *Pastoral Psychology* 18 (Oct. 1967): 18-24.

Mitford, J. *The American Way of Death*. New York: Simon & Schuster, 1963.

Morris, J. K. *Premarital Counseling: A Manual for Ministers*. Englewood Cliffs, N. J.: Prentice-Hall, 1960.

Mowrer, O. H. *The Crisis in Psychiatry and Religion*. New York: Van Nostrand, 1961.

— — — — . *Morality and Mental Health*. Chicago: Rand McNally, 1967.

— — — — . *The New Group Therapy*. New York: Litton, 1964.

Narramore, C. M. *The Psychology of Counseling*. Grand Rapids: Zondervan, 1960.

Nederhood, J. *Too Early to Marry*. Chicago: The Back-to-God Hour, 1963.

Oates, W. E. *Premarital Pastoral Care and Counseling*. Nashville: Broadman, 1958.

— — — — ., ed. *An Introduction to Pastoral Counseling*. Nashville: Broadman, 1959.

— — — — . "Making the Contact: Informal Pastoral Relationships" in *An Introduction to Pastoral Counseling*. Nashville: Broadman, 1959, pp. 69-80.

— — — — . *The Minister's Own Mental Health*. Great Neck, N. Y.: Channel, 1961.

Oates, W. E. and Lester, A. D. *Pastoral Care in Crucial Human Situations*. Valley Forge, Pa.: Judson, 1969.

Oglesby, W. B., Jr. *Referral in Pastoral Counseling*. Englewood Cliffs, N. J.: Prentice-Hall, 1968.

Packard, Vance. *Status Seekers*. New York: Simon & Schuster, Pocket Books, 1961.

Peterson, W. J. "What's the Future of the Sunday School?" *Eternity*, Part 1, vol. 19, no. 10 (Oct. 1968): 11-14; and Part 2, vol. 19, no. 11 (Nov. 1968): 15-17, 25-27, 37.

Porter, E. H., Jr., *An Introduction to Therapeutic Counseling*. Boston: Houghton Mifflin, 1950.

Proelss, E. F. "Ministering to the Physically Disabled Person," *Pastoral Psychology* 16 (June 1965): 8-22, 66.

Ramsey, G. V. "Group Marriage Counseling for Normal Young Marrieds," *Pastoral Psychology* 13 (Mar. 1962): 30-34.

Reid, C. *Groups Alive—Church Alive: The Effective Use of Small Groups in the Local Church*. New York: Harper & Row, 1969.

Richardson, A. *The Biblical Doctrine of Work*. London: SCM, 1952.

Robertson, J. *Young Children in Hospital*. London: Tavistock, 1958.

Robertson, R. N.; Maholick, L. T. and Shapiro, D. S. "The Parish Minister as Counselor: A Dilemma and Challenge," *Pastoral Psychology* 20 (June 1969): 24-30.

Rogers, W. F. "The Pastor's Work with Grief," *Pastoral Psychology* 14 (Sept. 1963): 19-26.

Rosenburg, M. *Occupations and Values.* Glencoe, Ill.: Free, 1957.

Rutledge, A. L. *Pre-marital Counseling.* Cambridge, Mass.: Schenkman, 1966.

Satir, V. *Cojoint Family Therapy.* Rev. ed. Palo Alto, Calif.: Science and Behavior Books, 1967.

Scherzer, C. J. *Ministering to the Dying.* Philadelphia: Fortress, 1967.

—————. *Design for Christian Marriage.* Westwood, N. J.: Revell, 1959.

Shea, T. "New Seminar Helps Take the Sting out of Death," *National Observer* (Jan. 5, 1970), p. 22.

Shertzer, B. and Stone, S. C. *Fundamentals of Counseling.* Boston: Houghton Mifflin, 1968.

—————. *Fundamentals of Guidance.* Boston: Houghton Mifflin, 1966.

Skinner, T. *Black and Free.* Grand Rapids: Zondervan, 1968.

Small, D. H. *After You've Said I Do.* Old Tappan, N. J.: Revell, 1968.

—————. *D sign for Christian Marriage.* Westwood, N. J.: Revell, 1959.

Smith, B. L. "Till Death Us Do Part?" *Christianity Today* 14 (Jan. 16, 1970): 5-10.

Soules, B. J. "Thalidomide Victims in a Rehabilitation Center," *American Journal of Nursing* 66 (Sept. 1966): 2023-26.

Southard, S. *Counseling for Church Vocations.* Nashville: Broadman, 1957.

Stewart, C. W. *The Minister as Marriage Counselor.* New York: McGraw-Hill, 1965.

Strommen, M. P. *Profiles of Church Youth.* St. Louis: Concordia, 1963.

Super, D. E. *The Psychology of Careers.* New York: Harper & Row, 1957.

Sutherland, R. I. and Smith, B. K., eds. *Understanding Mental Health.* Princeton, N. J.: Van Nostrand, 1965.

Szasz, Thomas. "The Myth of Mental Illness," *American Psychologist* 15 (1960): 113-18.

Teikmanis, A. L. *Preaching and Pastoral Care.* Philadelphia: Fortress, 1964.

Terkelsen, H. E. *Counseling the Unwed Mother.* Philadelphia: Fortress, 1964.

Terman, L. M. *Psychological Factors in Marital Happiness.* New York: McGraw-Hill, 1938.

Thieme, R. B., Jr. *The Biblical View of Sex, Love and Marriage.* Houston: Berachah Church, 1964.

Thompson, W. E. "Pre-retirement Anticipation and Adjustment in Retirement," *Journal of Social Issues* 14, no. 2 (1958): 35-45.

Thoroman, E. C. *The Vocational Counseling of Adults and Young People.* Boston: Houghton Mifflin, 1968.

Tweedie, D. F. *The Christian and the Couch: An Introduction to Christian Logotherapy.* Grand Rapids: Baker, 1963.

Udry, J. R. *The Social Context of Marriage.* Philadelphia: Lippincott, 1966.

Weisskopf-Joelson, Edith. "Psychology and the Insights of Religion." Paper read at First Unitarian Church, Cincinnati (Nov. 13, 1959).

Weits, H. "Guidance as Behavioral Change," *American Personnel and Guidance Journal* (Mar. 1961), pp. 558-59.

Whitlock, G. E. "The Role of the Minister in Vocational Counseling," *Pastoral Psychology* 12 (Sept. 1961): 14-22.

Williamson, E. G. "Value Orientation in Counseling" in *Humanistic Viewpoints in Psychology*, ed. F. T. Severin. New York: McGraw-Hill, 1965, pp. 359-77.

Wismer, E. "Small Groups and Church Renewal," *Pastoral Psychology* 18 (Mar. 1967): 7-13.

Wolff, S. *Children Under Stress*. London: Allen Lane, Penguin Book, 1969.

Womble, D. L. *Foundations for Marriage and Family Relations*. New York: Macmillan, 1966.

Wright, B. A. *Physical Disability—A Psychological Approach*. New York: Harper & Row, 1960.

Zuck, R. B. and Getz, G. A. *Christian Youth: An In-Depth Study*. Chicago: Moody, 1968.

# INDEX

## A

## B

## C

196

# D

# E

# F

# N

needs  22, 33, 35, 92, 93, 122, 144, 146-8, 153, 160, 174, 176
neurosis, neurotic  57, 92, 162, 170
note taking  36, 37
nude therapy  64

# O

objectivity  39
opinions  19, 96
optimism  18
overinvolvement  39

# P

pain  138, 142, 148, 158
panic  88
pastors  9, 10, 11, 29, 41, 53, 54, 55, 62, 66, 67, 69, 71, 82, 85, 102, 105,
    107, 113, 114, 117, 118, 124, 126, 127, 141, 142, 144, 153, 154, 169, 171
pastoral counseling (see counseling, pastoral)
pastoral psychology  67
patience  18, 33, 156
peace  33, 143, 149, 167
personality  37, 54, 55, 95, 111, 171
physical contact  38
physical disability  88, 151-5, 158
praise  33, 51
prayer  14, 22, 31, 32, 34, 39, 40, 50, 51, 53, 64, 84, 100, 104, 114, 125,
    134, 139, 141, 144, 146, 174, 175, 176, 181
preaching  174
pregnant, pregnancy  50, 73, 84, 86, 100, 167
prejudice  78
premarital counseling (see counseling, premarital)
prevention of abnormality  159, 167-171, 181
pride  51, 91
probing  28, 30
problems  11, 17, 19, 20, 21, 22, 23, 26, 32, 33, 39, 41, 46, 47, 50, 51, 52,
    53, 58, 63, 65, 68, 69, 72, 73, 77, 95, 96, 102, 106, 120, 129, 131, 132,
    134, 147, 154, 157, 165, 169, 170, 172, 175, 177, 178, 180, 181
  emotional  54, 159
  family  71, 72, 103, 104
  marital  71, 72, 73, 85, 88-102, 104
  personal  9, 13, 54, 175
  psychological  60
  spiritual  60

# T

# U

# V

# W